RELIGIONS
OF THE
WORLD

BUDDHISM

CHRISTIANITY

CONFUCIANISM

HINDUISM

ISLAM

JUDAISM

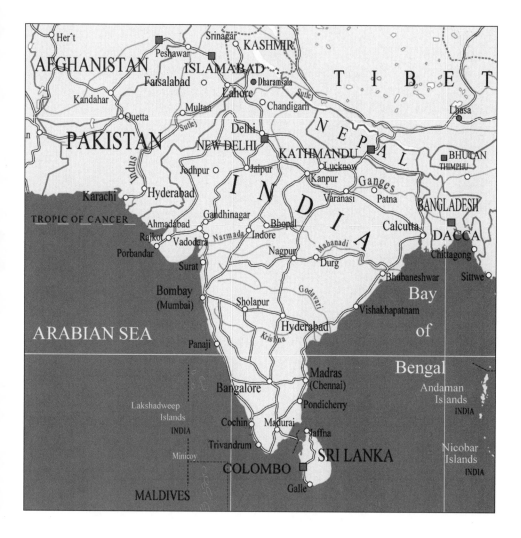

RELIGIONS
OF THE
WORLD

HINDUISM

James B. Robinson
Professor of Religion,
University of Northern Iowa

Series Consulting Editor **Ann Marie B. Bahr**
Professor of Religious Studies,
South Dakota State University

Foreword by **Martin E. Marty**
Professor Emeritus,
University of Chicago Divinity School

CHELSEA HOUSE
PUBLISHERS
A Haights Cross Communications Company

Philadelphia

FRONTIS Its sheer size makes the Indian subcontinent a major influence in world affairs. Because Hindus make up over 80 percent of this massive nation's population, Hinduism, too, is one of the world's most populous religions.

CHELSEA HOUSE PUBLISHERS

VP, NEW PRODUCT DEVELOPMENT Sally Cheney
DIRECTOR OF PRODUCTION Kim Shinners
CREATIVE MANAGER Takeshi Takahashi
MANUFACTURING MANAGER Diann Grasse

Staff for HINDUISM

EXECUTIVE EDITOR Lee Marcott
SENIOR EDITOR Tara Koellhoffer
PRODUCTION EDITOR Megan Emery
ASSOCIATE PHOTO EDITOR Noelle Nardone
SERIES AND COVER DESIGNER Keith Trego
LAYOUT 21st Century Publishing and Communications, Inc.

A Haights Cross Communications ◀ Company

www.chelseahouse.com

First Printing

9 8 7 6 5 4 3 2 1

Library of Congress Cataloging-in-Publication Data

Robinson, James B. (James Burnell), 1944–
  Hinduism/James B. Robinson.
    p. cm.—(Religions of the world)
Includes bibliographical references and index.
  ISBN 0-7910-7858-2 HC   0-7910-8013-7 PB
  1. Hinduism—Juvenile literature. [1. Hinduism.] I. Title. II. Series.
BL1203.R63 2004
294.5—dc22

                                                        2003025618

CONTENTS

Foreword

On this very day, like all other days, hundreds of millions of people around the world will turn to religion for various purposes.

On the one hand, there are purposes that believers in any or all faiths, as well as unbelievers, might regard as positive and benign. People turn to religion or, better, to their own particular faith, for the experience of healing and to inspire acts of peacemaking. They want to make sense of a world that can all too easily overwhelm them because it so often seems to be meaningless and even absurd. Religion then provides them with beauty, inspires their souls, and impels them to engage in acts of justice and mercy.

To be informed citizens of our world, readers have good reason to learn about these features of religions that mean so much to so many. Those who study the faiths do not have to agree with any of them and could not agree with all of them, different as they are. But they need basic knowledge of religions to understand other people and to work out strategies for living with them.

On the other hand—and religions always have an "other hand"—believers in any of the faiths, and even unbelievers who are against all of them, will find their fellow humans turning to their religions for purposes that seem to contradict all those positive features. Just as religious people can heal and be healed, they can also kill or be killed in the name of faith. So it has been through history.

This killing can be literal: Most armed conflicts and much terrorism today are inspired by the stories, commands, and promises that come along with various faiths. People can and do read and act upon scriptures that can breed prejudice and that lead them to reject other beliefs and believers. Or the killing can be figurative, which means that faiths can be deadening to the spirit. In the name of faith, many people are repressed, oppressed, sometimes victimized and abused.

If religion can be dangerous and if it may then come with "Handle with Care" labels, people who care for their own security, who want to lessen tensions and inspire concord, have to equip themselves by learning something about the scriptures and stories of their own and other faiths. And if they simply want to take delight in human varieties and imaginings, they will find plenty to please them in lively and reliable accounts of faiths.

A glance at television or at newspapers and magazines on almost any day will reveal stories that display one or both sides of religion. However, these stories usually have to share space with so many competing accounts, for example, of sports and entertainment or business and science, that writers and broadcasters can rarely provide background while writing headlines. Without such background, it is hard to make informed judgments.

The series RELIGIONS OF THE WORLD is designed to provide not only background but also rich illustrative material about the foreground, presenting the many features of faiths that are close at hand. Whoever reads all eleven volumes will find that these religions have some elements in common. Overall, one can deduce that their followers take certain things with ultimate seriousness: human dignity, devotion to the sacred, the impulse to live a moral life. Yet few people are inspired by religions in general. They draw strength from what they hold particularly. These particulars of each faith are not always contradictory to those of others, but they are different in important ways. It is simply a fact that believers are informed and inspired by stories told in separate and special ways.

A picture might make all this vivid: Reading about a religion, visiting a place of worship, or coming into the company of those who believe in and belong to a particular faith, is like entering a room. Religions are, in a sense, spiritual "furnished apartments." Their adherents have placed certain pictures on the wall and moved in with their own kind of furnishings, having developed their special ways of receiving or blocking out light from such places. Some of their figurative apartments are airy, and some stress strength and security.

Philosopher George Santayana once wrote that, just as we do not speak language, we speak particular languages, so we have religion not as a whole but as religions "in particular." The power of each living and healthy religion, he added, consists in "its special and surprising message and in the bias which that revelation gives to life." Each creates "another world to live in."

The volumes in this series are introductions to several spiritual furnished apartments, guides to the special and surprising messages of these large and complex communities of faith, or religions. These are not presented as a set of items in a cafeteria line down which samplers walk, tasting this, rejecting that, and moving on. They are not bids for window-shoppers or shoppers of any sort, though it may be that a person without faith might be drawn to one or another expression of the religions here described. The real intention of the series is to educate.

Education could be dull and drab. Picture a boring professor standing in front of a class and droning on about distant realities. The authors in this series, however, were chosen because they can bring readers up close to faiths and, sometimes better, to people of faith; not to religion but to people who are religious in particular ways.

As one walks the streets of a great metropolis, it is not easy and may not even be possible to deduce what are the faith-commitments of those one passes unless they wear a particular costume, some garb or symbol prescribed by their faith. There-fore, while passing them by, it is not likely that one can learn much about the dreams and hopes, the fears and intentions, of those around them.

These books, in effect, stop the procession of passersby and bid visitors to enter those sanctuaries where communities worship. Each book could serve as a guide to worship. Several years ago, a book called *How to Be a Perfect Stranger* offered brief counsel on how to feel and to be at home among worshipers from other traditions. This series recognizes that we are not strangers to each other only in sanctuaries. We carry over our attachments to conflicting faiths where we go to work or vote or serve in the military or have fun. These "carryovers" tend to come from the basic stories and messages of the several faiths.

The publishers have taken great pains to assign their work to authors of a particular sort. Had these been anti-religious or anti–the religion about which they write, they would have done a disservice. They would, in effect, have been blocking the figurative doors to the faiths or smashing the furniture in the sanctuaries. On the other hand, it would be wearying and distorting had the assignment gone to public relations agents, advertisers who felt called to claim "We're Number One!" concerning the faith about which they write.

Fair-mindedness and accuracy are the two main marks of these authors. In rather short compass, they reach a wide range of subjects, focusing on everything one needs to advance basic understanding. Their books are like mini-encyclopedias, full of information. They introduce the holidays that draw some neighbors to be absent from work or school for a day or a season. They include galleries of notable figures in each faith-community.

Since most religions in the course of history develop different ways in the many diverse places where they thrive, or because they attract intelligent, strong-willed leaders and writers, they come up with different emphases. They divide and split off into numberless smaller groups: Protestant and Catholic and Orthodox Christians, Shiite and Sunni Muslims, Orthodox and Reform Jews, and many kinds of Buddhists and Hindus. The writers in this series do justice to these variations, providing a kind of map without which one will get lost in the effort to understand.

Some years ago, a rabbi friend, Samuel Sandmel, wrote a book about his faith called *The Enjoyment of Scriptures*. What an astonishing concept, some might think: After all, religious scriptures deal with desperately urgent, life-and-death-and-eternity issues. They have to be grim and those who read them likewise. Not so. Sandmel knew what the authors of this series also know and impart: that the journeys of faith and the encounter with the religions of others include pleasing and challenging surprises. I picture many a reader coming across something on these pages that at first looks obscure or forbidding, but then, after a slightly longer look, makes sense and inspires an "aha!" There are many occasions for "aha-ing!" in these books. One can also wager that many a reader will come away from the encounters thinking, "I never knew that!" or "I never thought of that before." And they will be more ready than they had been to meet strangers of other faiths in a world that so many faiths *have* to share, or that they *get* to share.

Martin E. Marty
The University of Chicago

Preface

The majority of people, both in the United States and around the world, consider religion to be an important part of their lives. Beyond its significance in individual lives, religion also plays an important role in war and peace, politics, social policy, ethics, and cultural expression. Yet few people feel well-prepared to carry on a conversation about religion with friends, colleagues, or their congressional delegation. The amount of knowledge people have about their own faith varies, but very few can lay claim to a solid understanding of a religion other than their own. As the world is drawn closer together by modern communications, and the religions of the world jostle each other in religiously plural societies, the lack of our ability to dialogue about this aspect of our lives results in intercultural conflict rather than cooperation. It means that individuals of different religious persuasions will either fight about their faiths or avoid the topic of religion altogether. Neither of these responses aids in the building of healthy, religiously plural societies. This gap in our knowledge is therefore significant, and grows increasingly more significant as religion plays a larger role in national and international politics.

The authors and editors of this series are dedicated to the task of helping to prepare present and future decision-makers to deal with religious pluralism in a healthy way. The objective scholarship found in these volumes will blunt the persuasive power of popular misinformation. The time is short, however. Even now, nations are dividing along religious lines, and "neutral" states as well as partisan religious organizations are precariously, if not always intentionally, tipping delicate balances of power in favor of one religious group or another with doles of aid and support for certain policies or political leaders. Intervention in the affairs of other nations is always a risky business, but doing it without understanding of the religious sensitivities of the populace dramatically increases the chances that even well-intentioned intervention will be perceived as political coercion or cultural invasion. With such signs of ignorance already manifest, the day of reckoning for educational policies that ignore the study of the world's religions cannot be far off.

This series is designed to bring religious studies scholarship to the leaders of today and tomorrow. It aims to answer the questions that students, educators, policymakers, parents, and citizens might have about the new religious milieu in which we find ourselves. For example, a person hearing about a religion that is foreign to him or her might want answers to questions like these:

- How many people believe in this religion? What is its geographic distribution? When, where, and how did it originate?

- What are its beliefs and teachings? How do believers worship or otherwise practice their faith?

- What are the primary means of social reinforcement? How do believers educate their youth? What are their most important communal celebrations?

- What are the cultural expressions of this religion? Has it inspired certain styles of art, architecture, literature, or music? Conversely, does it avoid art, literature, or music for religious reasons? Is it associated with elements of popular culture?

- How do the people who belong to this religion remember the past? What have been the most significant moments in their history?

- What are the most salient features of this religion today? What is likely to be its future?

We have attempted to provide as broad coverage as possible of the various religious forces currently shaping the planet. Judaism, Christianity, Islam, Hinduism, Buddhism, Confucianism, Taoism, Sikhism, and Shinto have each been allocated an entire volume. In recognition of the fact that many smaller ancient and new traditions also exercise global influence, we present coverage of some of these in two additional volumes titled "Indigenous Religions" and "New Religions." Each volume in the series discusses demographics and geography, founder or foundational period, scriptures, worldview, worship or practice, growing up in the religion, cultural expressions, calendar and holidays, history, and the religion in the world today.

The books in this series are written by scholars. Their approach to their subject matter is neutral and objective. They are not trying to convert readers to the religion they are describing. Most scholars, however, value the religion they have chosen to study, so you can expect the general tone of these books to be appreciative rather than critical.

Religious studies scholars are experts in their field, but they are not critics in the same sense in which one might be an art, film, or literary critic. Religious studies scholars feel obligated to describe a tradition faithfully and accurately, and to interpret it in a way that will allow nonbelievers as well as believers to grasp its essential structure, but they do not feel compelled to pass judgment on it. Their goal is to increase knowledge and understanding.

Academic writing has a reputation for being dry and uninspiring. If so, religious studies scholarship is an exception. Scholars of religion have the happy task of describing the words and deeds of some of the world's most amazing people: founders, prophets, sages, saints, martyrs, and bodhisattvas.

The power of religion moves us. Today, as in centuries past, people thrill to the ethical vision of Confucianism, or the dancing beauty of Hinduism's images of the divine. They are challenged by the one, holy God of the Jews, and comforted by the saving promise of Christianity. They are inspired by the stark purity of

Islam, by the resilience of tribal religions, by the energy and innovation of the new religions. The religions have retained such a strong hold on so many people's lives over such a long period of time largely because they are unforgettable.

Religious ideas, institutions, and professions are among the oldest in humanity's history. They have outlasted the world's great empires. Their authority and influence have endured far beyond that of Earth's greatest philosophers, military leaders, social engineers, or politicians. It is this that makes them so attractive to those who seek power and influence, whether such people intend to use their power and influence for good or evil. Unfortunately, in the hands of the wrong person, religious ideas might as easily be responsible for the destruction of the world as for its salvation. All that stands between us and that outcome is the knowledge of the general populace. In this as in any other field, people must be able to critically assess what they are being told.

The authors and editors of this series hope that all who seek to wield the tremendous powers of religion will do so with unselfish and noble intent. Knowing how unlikely it is that that will always be the case, we seek to provide the basic knowledge necessary to critically assess the degree to which contemporary religious claims are congruent with the history, scriptures, and genius of the traditions they are supposed to represent.

Ann Marie B. Bahr
South Dakota State University

1

Introduction to Hinduism

*This very same ancient science of uniting the
individual consciousness with the Ultimate Consciousness
and which is the supreme secret;
therefore is being described by Me unto you
today because you are My devotee and friend.*

—Bhagavad Gita

India, the largest country in South Asia, occupies a distinct landmass that presses up hard against the mainland of Asia. This geological pressure forces land upward to form the highest mountain range in the world—the Himalayas. For this reason, India is often referred to as a "subcontinent." Its sheer size makes the Indian subcontinent a place of great importance.

India is also the home of one of the major ancient civilizations in the world and, with it, one of the world's oldest religions—Hinduism. Hinduism is a fascinating religious tradition but one that differs in many ways from what people in the Western world normally think of as religion. Indeed, Hinduism is so rich and varied that some scholars have suggested that we ought to think of it as a family of religions rather than as a single religious system.

A DEFINITION OF HINDUISM

Hinduism was actually given its name by people from outside India. Muslim invaders from the West referred to the people and culture of India as *Hindu,* which literally means "those across the Indus River"—a very important river system that runs through northwest India and present-day Pakistan. The Indus has often served as an informal boundary between India and Central Asia. Adding the "-ism" simply designates the beliefs and practices of those people called Hindus.

The Hindus themselves use the term *sanatana Dharma* to describe their religion. It means "the everlasting Law." This word *dharma,* which refers to a person's proper station in life, is one of the key concepts of Hinduism.

Most Hindus would not define their religion in terms of a single creed that embodies the faith because different Hindus may believe in many different things. However, certain characteristics do recur frequently within the wide spectrum of beliefs in the Hindu religion, and this allows us to view Hinduism as a whole.

The first characteristic that Hindus share is a regard for the *Vedas* (the earliest sacred Hindu texts) as inspired and divine, even though believers vary widely in how they interpret and use the Vedas in their own lives. Some, like members of the Hindu reform movement called the *Arya Samaj*, make the Vedic literature central to their religious outlook. Others, no less Hindu, scarcely use the actual Vedic texts at all and instead rely more heavily on later literature. Whatever the role of the ancient Vedas in daily practice, all Hindus would affirm that the texts are central to Hinduism.

A second characteristic that pervades Hinduism is the doctrine of *karma* and *reincarnation*. Simply put, Hindus believe that after death, human beings are reborn into different bodies over and over again, a process called reincarnation. The quality of life we encounter in those future incarnations depends on how we act in our present lives, in the here and now. The force or impact of these present-day actions on future lives is called karma.

A third characteristic common to all Hindus is the belief in a social class system associated with the stages of life. Controversial as it is, the *caste system*—a strict hierarchical division of society in which everyone is born to a particular rank that can not be changed in the present life—serves as a unifying force in the Hindu vision of society.

Thus, rather than being characterized as an overall spiritual concept or belief, Hinduism is more easily defined in terms of what its followers *do*—their rituals, ceremonies, family practices—and the caste system that organizes their society. In fact, Hindu society is a rich network of mutual duties and responsibilities that create a very cohesive community. It would not be wrong to say that "Hindu is as Hindu does."

One essentially has to be born Hindu in order to be considered a Hindu by others. This means that Hinduism is an *ethnocentric* religion—a faith intended for a particular set of people and for a particular culture. Western religions, on the other hand, are *universal*; they are intended to include everybody in the world. Although many Westerners share beliefs similar to those of the Hindus, this does not make them Hindus in the eyes of the

(Continued on page 8)

BASIS OF THE CASTE SYSTEM

The caste system of India actually had its origins in the sacred writings of the Bhagavad Gita, although some scholars argue that the hierarchical society put into place was an abuse of what the Gita meant when it said there are four orders of human beings: Brahman, Kshatriyas, Vaisyas, and Sudras.

The Bhagavad Gita says in Chapter Four, Verse Thirteen:

The Lord says:

"The fourfold caste has been created by Me
according to the differentiation of Guna and Karma."

Chapter Eighteen, Verse Forty says:

"There is no being on earth, or again in heaven among the
gods, that is liberated from the three qualities born of Nature."

Chapter Eighteen, Verse Forty-one says:

"Of Brahmanas, Kshtriyas and Vaishyas, as also the Sudras,
O Arjuna, the duties are distributed according to the qualities
born of their own nature."

The Mahabharata Santi Parva explained:

Brigu said, ". . . (The Creator created) human beings with their four divisions, viz., Brahmanas, Kshatriyas, Vaisyas, and Sudras. The complexion the Brahmanas obtained was white; that which the Kshatriyas obtained was red; that which the Vaisyas got was yellow; and that which was given to the Sudras was black."

[The words expressive of hue or colour really refer to attributes. What is intended to be said is that the Brahmanas had the attribute of Goodness (Sattwa); the second order had the attribute of Passion (Rajas); the third got a mixture of the two, i.e., both goodness and passion (Sattwa and Rajas); while the lowest order got the remaining attribute, viz., Darkness (Tamas).]

Bharadwaja said, "If the distinction between the four orders of human beings be made by means only of colour (attribute), then it seems that all the four orders have been mingled together. Lust, wrath, fear, cupidity, grief, anxiety, hunger, toil,—possess and prevail over all men. How can men be distinguished by the possession of attributes? The bodies of all men emit sweat, urine, faeces, phlegm, bile, and blood. How then can men be distributed into classes? Of mobile objects the number is infinite; the species also of immobile objects are innumerable. How then, can, objects of such very great diversity be distributed into classes?"

Brigu said, "There is really no distinction between the different orders. The whole world at first consisted of Brahmanas. Created equal by the Creator, men have in consequence of their acts, become distributed into different orders. They that became fond of indulging in desire and enjoying pleasures, possessed of the attributes of severity and wrath, endued with courage, and unmindful of the duties of piety and worship,—these Brahmanas possessing the attribute of Passion,—became Kshatriyas.

Those Brahmanas again who, without attending to the duties laid down for them, became possessed of both the attributes of Goodness and Passion, and took to the professions of cattle-rearing and agriculture, became Vaisyas. Those Brahmanas again that became fond of untruth and injuring other creatures, possessed of cupidity,—engaged in all kinds of acts for a living, and fallen away from purity of behaviour, and thus wedded to the attribute of Darkness, became Sudras.

Separated by these occupations, Brahmanas, falling away from their own order, became members of the other three orders. All the four orders, therefore, have always the right to the performance of all pious duties and of sacrifices. Even thus were the four orders at first created equal by Brahma (the Creator) who ordained for all of them (the observances disclosed in) the words of Brahma (in the Vedas). Through cupidity alone, many fell away, and became possessed by ignorance.

The Brahmanas always devoted to the scriptures on Brahma; and mindful of vows and restraints, are capable of grasping the conception of Brahman. Their penances therefore, never go for nothing. They amongst them are not Brahmanas

that are incapable of understanding that every created thing is Supreme Brahman. These, falling away, became members of diverse (inferior) orders. Losing the light of knowledge, and betaking themselves to an unrestrained course of conduct, they take birth as Pisachas and Rakshasas (demons) and Pretas and as individuals of diverse Mleccha species.

The great Rishis who at the beginning sprang into life (through the Creator's will) subsequently created, by means of their penances, men devoted to the duties ordained for them and attached to the rites laid down in the Eternal Vedas. That other Creation, however, which is eternal and undecaying, which is based upon Supreme Brahman and has sprung from the Primeval God, and which has its refuge upon yoga, is a mental one."

Bharadwaja said: "By what acts does one become a Brahman? By what a Kshatriya? By what acts again does one become a Vaisya or a Sudra? Tell me this, O foremost of speakers."

Brigu said, "That person is called a Brahman who has been sanctified by such rites as those called JATA and others; who is pure in behaviour; who is engaged in studying the Vedas; who is devoted to the six well-known acts (of ablutions every morning and evening, silent recitation of mantras, pouring libations on the sacrificial fire, worshiping the deities, doing the duties of hospitality to guests, and offering food to the Viswedevas); who is properly observant of all pious acts; who never takes food without having offered it duly to gods and guests; who is filled with reverence for his preceptor; and who is always devoted to vows and truth.

He is called a Brahmana in whom are truth, gifts, abstention from injury to others, compassion, shame, benevolence and penance.

He who is engaged in the profession of battle, who studies the Vedas, who makes gifts (to Brahmanas) and takes wealth (from those he protects) is called a Kshatriya.

He who earns fame from keep of cattle, who is employed in agriculture and the means of acquiring wealth, who is pure in behaviour and attends to the study of the Vedas, is called a Vaisya.

He who takes pleasure in eating every kind of food, who

is engaged in doing every kind of work, who is impure in behaviour, who does not study the Vedas, and whose conduct is unclean, is said to be a Sudra.

If these characteristics be observable in a Sudra, and if they be not found in a Brahmana, then such a Sudra, is no Sudra, and such a Brahmana is no Brahmana. By every means should cupidity and wrath be restrained.

This as also self-restraint, are the highest results of Knowledge. Those passions (cupidity and wrath), should, with one's whole heart, be resisted. They make their appearance for destroying one's highest good.

One should always protect one's prosperity from one's wrath, one's penance from pride; one's knowledge from honour and disgrace; and one's soul from error.

That intelligent person, who does all acts without desire of fruit, whose whole wealth exists for charity, and who performs the daily Homa, is a real renouncer (*karma-sannyasa*).

One should conduct oneself as a friend to all creatures, abstaining from all acts of injury. Rejecting the acceptance of all gifts, one should, by the aid of one's intelligence, be a complete master of one's passions. One should live in one's soul where there can be no grief. One would then have no fear here and attain to a fearless region hereafter. One should live always devoted to penances, and with all passions completely restrained; observing the vow of taciturnity, and with soul concentrated on itself; desirous of conquering the unconquered senses, and unattached in the midst of attachments.

The indications of a Brahmana are purity, good behaviour and compassion unto all creatures."*

* Source: From The Mahabharata-Santi Parva Section CLXXXVIII

(Continued from page 4)

Hindu community, for the simple reason that these Westerners were not born into the Hindu community.

HINDUISM IN THE WORLD

The fact that one must be born Hindu to be considered an adherent of the faith has not prevented Hinduism from becoming one of the major religions of the world. About 760 million people worldwide—including over 80 percent of the population of India—are Hindu.[1] This makes it the world's third-largest religion. (Only Islam and Christianity are larger.) Just as important, Hinduism continues to be a vital force among people of Indian descent living outside India. Hindus are to be found in Africa, North and South America, and in Europe—anywhere that people from India settled and made a home.

There are many Hindus in the United States, although they usually keep a low cultural profile. The Pluralism Project at Harvard University estimates that there are more than one million Hindus in America. The same study lists approximately 680 Hindu temples in the United States. California alone has over one hundred temples, and New York and New Jersey both have more than fifty temples. There is at least one Hindu temple in every state except Montana, Wyoming, North Dakota, South Dakota, and Iowa. [2]

DIFFERENT PATHS OF HINDUISM

Hinduism is made up of three great religious forms and three broad streams that continually flow and mingle together. The three great forms of Hinduism are *polytheism*, the worship of many gods; *monism*, the concept of seeking union with that "One Spirit" beyond the world and self; and finally, *monotheism*, which is worship that concentrates on "One Personal God."

The first stream of Hinduism is the *way of works*, which emphasizes performing proper ritual and doing one's duty in society. The second stream is the *way of knowledge*, the path of the mystic who seeks unity with the eternal. The third and most popular stream is the *way of devotion*, the path of those who put their faith in a personal god.

There are no real denominations within Hinduism as there are, for example, in Christianity. The fact that different people worship different gods is taken for granted. Hindus believe that all the gods and goddesses are really different expressions of one God, and that any form of Hinduism, if practiced sincerely, will

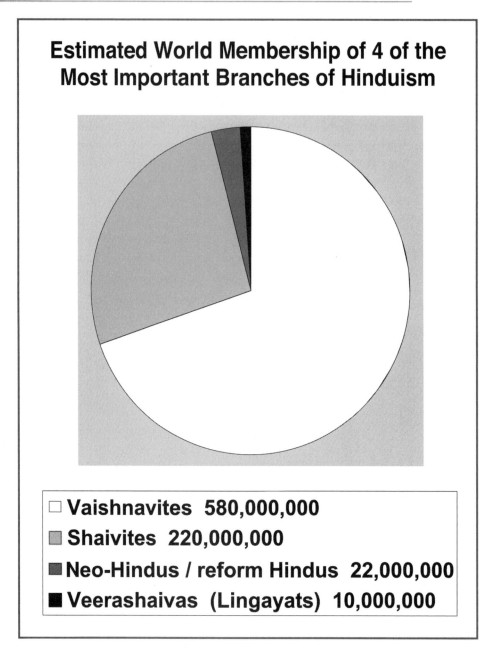

Estimated World Membership of 4 of the Most Important Branches of Hinduism

☐ **Vaishnavites 580,000,000**

▨ **Shaivites 220,000,000**

▨ **Neo-Hindus / reform Hindus 22,000,000**

■ **Veerashaivas (Lingayats) 10,000,000**

This pie chart shows the estimated membership of four major branches of Hinduism. By far the most numerous are Vaishnavites, or those who worship Vishnu.

bring about release from this world of pain and suffering. This release is called *moksha*.

If the essence of Hinduism could be summarized in a few words, those words might be "structured diversity." We might think of Hinduism as a rainbow in which all the different colors are represented, but in which each of these colors has a very distinct place in the spectrum. Both the diversity and the structuring are essential to the Hindu outlook on life. One of Hinduism's most unique characteristics is its acknowledgment that human beings are different not only from each other but at various times within their individual lives as well. Perhaps no other religion is so aware of the different conditions and types of humanity. Examples of almost every type of religious activity in the world may be found in some form somewhere in Hinduism.

2

Foundations
of Hinduism

Hinduism has no . . . single founder. Some modern
sociologists have defined Christians and Muslims
as those who consider themselves such, but a similar
definition cannot be applied to Hindus, for many
of them have scarcely heard the word Hindu, and
have no name for their own religion.

—A.L. Basham

THE SIGNIFICANCE OF THE VEDAS

Judaism, Christianity, and Islam can point to important individuals (Abraham, Moses, Jesus, and Muhammad) who served as the founders of their faith. Hindus have no one historical figure who stands at the beginning of their religion. The foundation of Hinduism is a body of texts called "the Vedas." Though Hinduism has many sacred texts, only the Vedas are called *shruti* ("that which is heard"). Non-Vedic sacred literature is called *smriti* ("that which is remembered"). The word *shruti* points to the direct contact with the divine that resulted in the Vedas.

The Vedas were revealed to *rishis*, a word that means "seer." (It may be no more than coincidence, but it is interesting to note that the earliest word for a prophet in the Hebrew Scriptures also means "seer.") Hindus believe that the rishis *saw* the truths that are contained in the Vedas; they did not invent or create them out of their own minds. For that reason, the Vedas are considered to be *apaurusheya* (impersonal, entirely superhuman). They are revelation.

The word *Veda* comes from the Sanskrit root *vid*, meaning "to know." *Veda* means "knowledge." Sanskrit, the sacred language of Hinduism, is a distant relative of English. Both are Indo-European languages. For that reason, we can find words in English that are related to the Sanskrit word *Veda*, such as *wit*, *wisdom*, and even *video*. Related words in different languages are called "cognates."

The Vedas are believed to be eternal, without beginning or end. They are not simply written texts. Hindus believe that they came out of the breath of God and are filled with eternal spiritual truths, or divine knowledge, which can never be destroyed. This seems to be a similar concept to that of biblical inspiration, which claims that the scriptures are "God-breathed."

Not all Hindus would say that the Vedas are "God-breathed," though many would, for most Hindus believe in a personal God. However, some Hindus refer to the divine as *Brahman*, a term for ultimate reality thought of as that which is beyond all designations of physical or personal attributes, and therefore impersonal. It is important to recognize that here *impersonal* means "not limited by personality," and therefore greater, not less, than something that is personal.

One is accepted as a Hindu whether one thinks of the ultimate reality as personal or impersonal. And no matter how one thinks of the divine, whether as a personal Lord or impersonal Brahman, all Hindus believe that the Vedas are divinely revealed. For Hinduism, one does not have to have a personal God to have revelation and scriptures.

Even though Hindus believe that the Vedas are more than written texts, we can still inquire into the historical origins of the written texts known as the Vedas. Where did the Vedas come from? We turn to that question in the next section.

THE ORIGINS OF THE VEDAS

In the late eighteenth century, Sanskrit was found to be similar to many European languages. This discovery gave birth to the concept of a family of languages known as Indo-European. English, French, German, Greek, Latin, Sanskrit, Russian, even Armenian and Gaelic, are all Indo-European languages. Linguists posit that all of these languages are descended from a single, proto-Indo-European language. But who were the speakers of this language, and where did they live?

Almost immediately, the quest for the Indo-European homeland became intertwined with the question of the supposed superiority and the inferiority of cultures. If India was the homeland, its culture would have to be acknowledged as the mother culture of the European nations. On the other hand, if Indo-Europeans were late arrivals in India, that might suggest that India received much of its culture from ancient Europe.

In the nineteenth century and the first half of the twentieth century, India was under British rule. It was the colonial period, and India was one of many British colonies. Although some British scholars admired India's culture, others were dedicated to the belief that colonial rule was justified because British culture was superior to Indian culture. Not surprisingly, the latter group favored the view that the original homeland was somewhere in Europe, and India was the recipient rather than the source of Indo-European language and culture. According to this model, the Indo-Europeans who settled in India were part of a vast movement of tribes out of the homeland, fanning out in all directions. These migrating tribes would eventually become the people we know as the Greeks, Latins, Celts, Germans, and Slavs.

According to the standard Western reconstruction of India's history, one group of Indo-European-speaking people traveled even farther from the original homeland. They traveled south and east to an area near the Caspian Sea, where they settled for an unknown amount of time before resuming their migration southward and eastward. One branch of this group moved into what is now India around the middle of the second millennium B.C., while another branch settled in what is now Iran. Both branches called themselves the *Aryans,* meaning "the noble people." Indeed, *Iran* comes from the same root as *Aryan.* Scholars refer to the branch that entered India as the "Indo-Aryans." They are presumed to have been tall and light-skinned, similar to modern Europeans.

The Indo-Aryans were warriors and nomads. They had horse-drawn chariots, cows, sheep, goats, and dogs. They overran the indigenous people of India, whom they called *Dasas.* It is not known for sure who the Dasas were, but some scholars think they were the remnants of the Indus Valley Civilization, which thrived between 2500 and 1500 B.C.

The invading Indo-Aryans brought with them the religious beliefs and practices described in the Vedas. In other words, according to the Western reconstruction of India's history, the Vedas arrived late in India, and reflected a nonindigenous religion. Vedic religion incorporated some elements of the indigenous religious beliefs as it developed in India, but its core was of foreign origin.

THE INDUS VALLEY CIVILIZATION

Around the turn of the twentieth century, archaeologists began to uncover evidence of an advanced culture that flourished in northwest India from around 2500 to around 1500 B.C.—that is, just prior to the posited time of arrival of the Indo-Aryans. As with other great civilizations, this one grew up along a river that served both as a water source and as a major artery of transport. In this case, the river was the Indus, so this culture is generally called the *Indus Valley Civilization.*

Evidence uncovered so far indicates that the Indus Valley people had a highly organized civilization with a number of cities. Major excavations have been at Harappa in the Punjab and Mohenjodaro in Sindh, both of which were fortified cities. These cities appear to have carried on extensive trade with Mesopotamia. Their sophisticated writing system, which bears no resemblance to any other script known to us, is one of the great historical mysteries. It has not yet been deciphered; we do not even know to which language family it belongs.

For reasons not fully understood, this civilization went into decline. Some believe that there may have been significant changes in climate, or there may have been major shifts in the flow of the all-important Indus River.

At one time, it was widely believed that the Indus Valley cities were overrun by invading Indo-Aryan peoples. Some Vedic hymns celebrate the conquest of indigenous peoples. They describe how Indra, the divine warrior, violently overthrows the fortresses of his enemies.

More recent evaluation of the archaeological evidence has cast some doubt on this once popular invasion and conquest theory. It now appears more likely that the Indus Valley Civilization had entered a period of decline before the Indo-Aryans arrived. Others believe that the migration of the Indo-Aryan peoples was more gradual and peaceful, and that it led to a process of assimilation rather than conquest.

We cannot say for certain to what degree the Indus Valley Civilization contributed to the development of Hinduism. As with other aspects of that culture, we can only try to reconstruct their religion on the basis of rather scant evidence.

The most common artifacts of the Indus Valley Civilization

are clay and soapstone seals. They are usually flat and square or rectangular sections of soapstone or shaped clay averaging about an inch on each side. They have scenes and inscriptions upon them that provide most of the samples of the script.

One intriguing figure appears on several of the seals. This figure wears a trident-shaped headdress, sits in a yogic posture, and is surrounded by animals. Though there are variant interpretations, the figure may have three faces, two of which are shown in profile. He appears to have an erect phallus (in Hindu terminology, a *lingam*).

Some scholars believe this figure may be a prototype for the later popular Hindu god Shiva. Shiva carries the trident suggested by the headdress. Shiva is called "Lord of Animals," which may correspond to the animals shown on the seals. Shiva is often shown sitting in a yogic posture as the figure on the seal seems to be doing. Shiva's religious emblem is the lingam. Thus, this figure is frequently called the "proto-Shiva" because many of the attributes of this Indus Valley figure might somehow have been transferred to the later Hindu god, Shiva.

THE SOCIETY OF THE INDO-ARYANS

The Indo-Aryan tribes were under the leadership of a hereditary chieftain called a *rajah* (cognate of the Latin word *rex*). As the Indo-Aryans acquired more territory and adopted a settled rather than a nomadic lifestyle, the functions of the rajah became more complex. He maintained his own private army to defend his people, as well as a cadre of priests to secure divine blessings for them.

Most of the settling tribesmen became farmers and herders. The father (*pitar*; cognates include Latin *pater*, German *vater*, and English *father*) was the head of the household and the owner of the family property. In the early Vedic period, he also served as the family priest.

The role of women in the Vedic Age is debated, but, at least in the early period, it appears that women enjoyed a relatively high degree of domestic authority and were not secluded. These freedoms may have been reserved for upper-class women, but, according to this

TAPAS (CREATIVE FERVOR)
Rig Veda X, 190

Translated by Raimon Panikkar

1. From blazing Ardor (*tapas*) Cosmic Order came and Truth;
   from thence was born the obscure night;
   from thence the ocean with its billowing waves.

2. From Ocean with its waves was born the year
   which marshals the succession of nights and days,
   controlling everything that blinks the eye.

3. Then, as before, did the creator fashion
   the Sun and Moon, the Heaven and Earth,
   the atmosphere and the domain of light.

Tapas (ardor), *rta* (order), and *satya* (truth) are important Hindu concepts. *Tapas* is the second to last hymn of the Rig Veda. *Tapas* means "ardor," "ascetic fire," "arduous penance," and "concentration." In this hymn, *tapas* is the energy that gives birth to cosmic order and to truth.

Rta is the structure or formal principle of reality. *Satya* is the content, the substance, the material principle of reality. Owing to *rta*, the world is a cosmos rather than a chaos, an ordered and harmonious whole rather than a jumbled, archaic soup. Owing to *satya*, the world is not merely a game or a deception. *Satya* is not primarily an epistemic truth but an ontic truthfulness—it is being what one appears to be. No reality can emerge without these two principles of *rta* and *satya*, of harmony and consistency.

The ocean represents space, and the year represents time. Once there is space and time, life (all that "blinks the eye") can appear, along with sun and moon, heaven and earth, etc.

In Hinduism, the renunciant who spends his days meditating is said to be performing *tapas*. The meditator is not idle; he is an active collaborator in the maintenance of the world. His ardor, energy, and power of concentration are believed to be capable of both creating and destroying the world.

Source: Raimon Panikkar, *The Vedic Experience*. Available online at
http://www.himalayanacademy.com/books/vedic_experience/Part1/VEPartIChA.html.

model, the Indo-Aryans *were* the upper class during the Vedic period. A wife and mother had authority over the household children and servants. She co-celebrated the domestic rites with her husband. Daughters were not censured for remaining unmarried, and they participated in the selection of a husband and the shaping of the marriage contract.[3]

Between 1500 and 500 B.C., the Vedas, originally oral literature, were gradually written down. During this same time period, public rites and sacrifices became more and more complicated. Philosophical speculation probed questions concerning the origins of the universe and its order. Although the Indo-Aryans did not have the rigid caste system of later India, the names of the four *varna* ("social classes": *Brahmins, Kshatriya, Vaishya,* and *Shudra*) appear in a Vedic hymn celebrating the creation of the cosmos.[4]

VEDIC RELIGION

The names of many deities, both male and female, appear in the *Rig Veda.* Most frequently mentioned is Indra, a god of war who was also associated with storms, especially the monsoon rains. He held in his hands a thunderbolt called a *vajra.*

Rudra was a mountain god associated with the destructive storms that swept down from the Himalayas. Awestruck, people beseeched him to be auspicious (*shiva*) rather than harmful. Indeed, Rudra did have a merciful side. In his mountain terrain, he presided over medicinal plants, and appeared at times as a gentle healer. In later Hinduism, the great god Shiva would inherit these complex, contradictory characteristics.

Other Vedic deities included Varuna, who upheld the laws of nature and the moral law, Vayu (the wind), and Surya (one of several sun gods). Agni, the fire god, served as the intermediary between the gods and humans through the sacrificial offering. There were female deities as well: Ushas (the dawn), the rivers Saraswati and Ganga, and Vac (the ritual power of speech).

Although Indra is the most frequently mentioned deity, the Vedic pantheon had no hierarchical order. Indeed, from the vantage point of Western theology, one of the most confusing things about the Vedas is their tendency to elevate each of the gods in turn to the highest rank. One after the other is lauded as creator and sole ruler of the universe. Everything that could be said of all the gods collectively is said of each one in turn. This is, strictly speaking, neither monotheism (for there are many gods) nor polytheism (for each god in turn absorbs all the others). Scholars call it *henotheism*, and describe it as the temporary elevation of one of many gods to the supreme position. Even at this earliest stage, India had a fluid theological system that offered no rigid boundaries between deities, and allowed for the supreme being to be called by many different names. Classical Hinduism would continue to espouse a similar theology.

INDRA

Although later supplanted by Vishnu and Shiva, Indra was a king of the gods during the Vedic Age. He was the god of thunder and storms, and a great warrior. He defended the heavens and the earth against the forces of evil. It was said he could revive warriors who had fallen in battle. His weapon was the *vajra* ("lightning bolt").

Indra's wife was Indrani, and his attendants were the Maruts. Two hundred fifty Rig Vedic hymns are dedicated to him, more than to any other god.

Indra's heavenly court was known as Svarga. It was located in the clouds surrounding the sacred mountain Meru, but Indra's heaven could move anywhere at his command. Svarga included an enormous hall where slain warriors went after death. Apsaras and Gandharvas danced and entertained the court. There were games and athletic contests as well.

Indra's most famous exploit was his victory over the demon Vrtra. Vrtra, who had assumed the form of a mighty dragon, had sealed off all the water in the world. This caused a terrible drought. Indra vowed to get back the life-giving waters. He rode forth to grapple with Vrtra. Indra had to destroy Vrtra's ninety-nine fortresses to find the dragon. The two clashed in a long battle, but Indra emerged the victor. The waters once again fell from the skies, and Indra became a great hero. The gods elected him to be their king.

Source: "Indra." *Encyclopedia Mythica* from Encyclopedia Mythica Online, http://www.pantheon.org/articles/i/indioa.html.

AN ALTERNATE INTERPRETATION OF THE VEDIC AGE

The aforementioned outline of ancient Indian history is found in all standard textbooks on the subject. Nonetheless, it is being challenged in India. A large element of the general populace, and a small but increasing number of Indian scholars, claim that the Vedic period ended around 3000 B.C., thereby preceding rather than following the Indus Valley Civilization (c. 2500–1500 B.C.). They also deny that there was an Indo-Aryan invasion. According to this group of scholars, both the Vedas and Vedic culture were indigenous to India. Hence, proponents of this model have been labeled "Indigenists."

This has become a highly politicized debate. Western Indologists, for the most part, do not take the Indigenist position seriously. They believe that claims of an indigenous Vedic culture are based on nationalism rather than on scholarship. Indigenist scholars, for their part, say that Western scholarship's refusal to seriously consider the Indigenist position is evidence of neocolonialist sentiments.

Edwin F. Bryant of Rutgers University has recently published the results of his efforts to disentangle the genuine scholarship from the polemics in this debate.[5] Although he is not at all certain that it will ever be substantiated, Bryant believes that the indigenous Aryan position cannot be ignored. Western scholars need to concede that it merits "a place at the table." On the other hand, Bryant believes that the Aryan invasion theory remains a reasonable way to account for much of the available evidence.

In sum, Bryant believes that both models can accommodate much of the evidence which is currently available. However, if the script on the Indus Valley seals is ever deciphered, that would tip the scales in one direction or the other. If the language on the seals is Indo-European, it would lend support to the Indigenist claim that Indo-Aryans were in India prior to the Indus Valley Civilization. If the language is not Indo-European, that would lend weight to the Indo-Aryan invasion hypothesis.

3

Sacred Scriptures in Hinduism

I worship the Gita.
The Gita ordains that one should
perform one's own duty. . . .

—Mohandas Gandhi

THE FOUR VEDAS

There are actually four collections of Vedic poetry—the Rig Veda, Sama Veda, Yajur Veda, and Atharva Veda. Each Vedic collection has four subdivisions: the *Samhitas*, which is the original collection of hymns, songs, or poetry; the "ritual texts," which explain how to carry out Vedic ceremonies; the "forest treatises," which are supposedly the spiritual writings of "forest dwellers"—hermits who have renounced the world; and last and probably most important for modern Hinduism, the *Upanishads*, which are the teachings of the great Hindu masters and show the path toward moksha (liberation from reincarnation).

Rig Veda Samhita

The Rig Veda Samhita is the most important of the hymn collections, reaching something approximating its present form in about 1000 B.C. It is not unlike the Book of Psalms in the Bible. It consists of 1,028 hymns organized into ten books. These hymns praise and glorify deities called *devas*, a word meaning "the Shining Ones" or "Beings of Light," suggesting entities filled with luminous sacred power.

The names of many devas suggest that these divine beings may originally have been personified natural forces: The name of the god *Agni*, for example, means "fire"—his name is related to the English word *ignite*; the name of the god *Surya* means "sun," *Vayu* means "wind," *Soma* is a sacred plant, and so forth. Female devas are hardly mentioned. The only one to have a hymn dedicated to her is *Ushas*, the "dawn."

These images drawn from nature over time acted like a seed crystal in a chemical solution. A wide variety of attributes, functions, and characteristics condensed around each nature god, and thus, the significance of the deity was broadened through analogy and metaphor. For example, Agni, the god of fire, is very important. The very first hymn of the Rig Veda identifies him as the priest among the devas. As the god of fire, he acts as a mediator between humankind and the gods, serving as the force that brings the burnt sacrificial offerings of humans up to the devas in heaven. He is the deva of the light of the fire, of truth, and so he becomes the guardian of the cosmic order. In other hymns, Agni is identified with the sun in the sky and lightning in the atmosphere. Agni comes to be everywhere.

The devas—superhuman sacred beings—are the gods and goddesses we associate with polytheism, or the worship of many

RIG VEDA—BOOK ONE
Hymn I. Agni.

1. I Laud Agni, the chosen Priest, God, minister of sacrifice,
   The hotar, lavishest of wealth.

2. Worthy is Agni to be praised by living as by ancient seers.
   He shall bring hitherward the Gods.

3. Through Agni man obtaineth wealth, yea, plenty waxing day by day,
   Most rich in heroes, glorious.

4. Agni, the perfect sacrifice which thou encompassest about
   Verily goeth to the Gods.

5. May Agni, sapient-minded Priest, truthful, most gloriously great,
   The God, come hither with the Gods.

6. Whatever blessing, Agni, thou wilt grant unto thy worshiper,
   That, Angiras, is indeed thy truth.

7. To thee, dispeller of the night, O Agni, day by day with prayer
   Bringing thee reverence, we come.

8. Ruler of sacrifices, guard of Law eternal, radiant One,
   Increasing in thine own abode.

9. Be to us easy of approach, even as a father to his son:
   Agni, be with us for our weal.

gods. In some ways, they are much like angels in the Western religions. However, angels serve a higher god; the very meaning of the word *angel* is "messenger." The devas do not serve a particular supreme being.

There are greater and lesser devas in the Vedic hymns. No one deity in the Vedas is regarded as the supreme being in the monotheistic sense. The most popular deva in the Rig Veda is Indra, the deva of storms and a war leader in heaven. His mightiest feat was to slay the dragon Vrtra and to release the life-giving waters that the dragon had hoarded. Above Indra is Varuna, the great god of the sky, who is a guardian of the moral order.

The early Vedic tradition points to *rita* (sometimes spelled *rta*), which means the "cosmic order," as the supreme ordering principle for god and human alike. Like many archaic conceptions of reality, rita expresses a dynamic view of how the world works. It was exemplified in the natural cycles of natural phenomena such as the sun, moon, planets, and seasons. The term *rita* is related to the English words *rite, ritual, right,* and *art.* The word eventually passed out of use and was replaced by the term *dharma,* which refers to the cosmic order and all its extensions in the natural order, the social order, and the moral order.

The many gods of Vedic polytheism have changed greatly over the centuries. Indra, Varuna, and Agni became less important, and gods that were once relatively minor, such as Vishnu and Rudra, who became Shiva, grew to have great importance in modern Hinduism. Unlike the God worshiped in faiths such as Islam and Christianity, none of the Hindu gods has declared, "Thou shalt have no other gods before me." The people of India are very comfortable with the idea that the divine is all around us, taking many different forms and answering to many different names.

Ritual Texts

The central religious activity in the Vedic religion is sacrifice. Sacrifice is a basic impulse that can be found in practice all over the world. To offer something to someone, even at a purely social level, is an attempt to enter into a special kind of relationship with the recipient. In whatever form it takes, sacrifice is a way of entering into a relationship with the divine.

In the earliest Vedic period, sacrifice was a way of connecting with the devas in order to win various worldly favors. Sacrifice might bring victory in battle, more cows and horses, fertile fields, or many sons, something valued in the Hindu culture. Various ritual texts, composed from about 1000 to 800 B.C., include descriptions of the great ceremonies and sacrifices. They describe not only how to carry out the physical acts of the rituals but also they stress the *bandhus* ("sacred connections"), or special relationships between sacrificial objects and the gods or cosmic powers. Using these sacred connections in a special kind of meditation, the sacrificer is said to be able to make the offering effective. In the ritual texts, it is sacrifice itself—not the devas—that is the central concern. The sacrifice can bring immortality and even divine status.

Like the devas, the idea of sacrifice evolved over the centuries. The notion that sacrifice was a means of acquiring spiritual power, however, remained constant. Such sacrifices might include offerings to the devas for rebirth or the sacrifice of pleasure and profit in order to follow a more virtuous life. Sacrifice can mean renouncing the world and devoting oneself to spiritual life, or the practice of harsh asceticism to gain such strong spiritual power that one becomes, for all practical purposes, equal to the devas themselves.

The Forest Treatises

The "forest treatises," which prescribe a certain type of meditation, were written at around 800–600 B.C.—a time when India was undergoing major social change. People were becoming more settled. Villages were evolving into larger towns and cities. A written script and a money-based economy made life much more complex than it had been before. Some religious people (mostly men but some women as well) saw life in the big cities as not very supportive of the religious life. They chose to leave the villages and went out into the forests. This pattern can still be found in Hinduism today when elderly people, having performed all their social requirements—having "paid their dues," so to speak—go into retirement and concentrate fully on their religious practices.

These forest-dwelling individuals did not have access to the Vedic sacrifices that were performed in the towns. Thus, with the help of the forest treatises, they used their imaginations to reconstruct the Vedic sacrifice in their minds. It was as if a contemporary Roman Catholic, forgoing traditional Mass, instead performed all the details of the Mass in his or her imagination, hoping for all the benefits that actual attendance would bring.

The *Upanishads*

Upanishads, which might be best translated as "private sessions," are texts containing what were once secret doctrines and practices passed down from a teacher (*guru*) to his disciples. Now these doctrines and practices are available to everyone. They were composed between 600 and 400 B.C., during a time when there was a radical shift in thinking, not only in India but all over the world. Some historians have called this "the axial age," meaning a time when the human mind turned, as on an axis, away from archaic, mythic thinking to more rational philosophical thought.

The Upanishads were not focused on the many Vedic gods in the Samhitas and the sacrifices offered to them. Because of this, they went beyond the sort of religion found in the earlier Vedic literature. Since the Upanishad texts are considered the culmination of the Vedic literature, they are called the *Vedanta*—the "end" or "pinnacle" of the Vedas—and the influential Vedanta philosophy, associated with the great thinker Shankara (788–820), is based on the Upanishads. Of all the Vedic texts, the Upanishads have been the most influential in both classical and modern Hinduism. English translations of them are readily available.

As in other parts of the world, Upanishadic men—and, again,

KENA-UPANISHAD:
First Khanda

1. The Pupil asks: "At whose wish does the mind sent forth proceed on its errand? At whose command does the first breath go forth? At whose wish do we utter this speech? What god directs the eye, or the ear?"

2. The Teacher replies: "It is the ear of the ear, the mind of the mind, the speech of speech, the breath of breath, and the eye of the eye. When freed (from the senses) the wise, on departing from this world, become immortal.

3. "The eye does not go thither, nor speech, nor mind. We do not know, we do not understand, how any one can teach it.

4. "It is different from the known, it is also above the unknown, thus we have heard from those of old, who taught us this.

5. "That which is not expressed by speech and by which speech is expressed, that alone know as Brahman, not that which people here adore.

6. "That which does not think by mind, and by which, they say, mind is thought, that alone know as Brahman, not that which people here adore.

7. "That which does not see by the eye, and by which one sees (the work of) the eyes, that alone know as Brahman, not that which people here adore.

8. "That which does not hear by the ear, and by which the ear is heard, that alone know as Brahman, not that which people here adore.

9. "That which does not breathe by breath, and by which breath is drawn, that alone know as Brahman, not that which people here adore."

a few women—looked to find "the one behind the many," the one divine behind the many devas, the one supreme power behind all the powers of the sacrifice. The Upanishadic thinkers were seeking the common denominator of all existence.

They finally settled upon *Brahman*, a term that might be translated as "Infinite Spirit," "Holy Power," or "the Eternal." This is the absolute being behind all changing phenomena. Brahma is not only the source but also the essential reality of all things.

On this subject, there is a decisive difference between Western religion and Hinduism. The ancient Israelites chose to concentrate on one god and to *exclude* all other gods. The Hindus, on the other hand, chose to concentrate on one god whose essence also *embraces* all other gods. For ancient Israel and later Western religions, the one god is the "supreme personal god," a creator who is above and beyond his creation. In the Upanishads, in contrast, the Infinite Spirit—from which all creation comes—fills and encompasses everything in nature and in self, rather than remaining a separate entity. The Infinite Spirit transcends all qualifications and attributes, including personality.

The technical term for a religion that centers on one being

THE HINDU IDEA OF CREATION

Sri Ramana Maharshi said:

> All metaphysical discussion is profitless unless it causes us to seek within the Self for the true reality.

> All controversies about creation, the nature of the universe, evolution, the purpose of God, etc., are useless. They are not conducive to our true happiness. People try to find out about things which are outside of them before they try to find out "Who am I?" Only by the latter means can happiness be gained. *

* Source: *The Teachings of Sri Ramana Maharshi*, ed. David Godman. Available online at http://www.hinduism.co.za/creation.htm#Creation.

beyond all personal attributes, infused with all of creation, is *monism*. In contrast, the religions of the West are all *monotheisms*, which means that they worship a God who is personal and stands above and beyond the world he made.

Brahman, or the Infinite Spirit, is at the very foundation of everything in Hinduism, which means that the Infinite Spirit is the basis of an individual's personal existence. At the core of one's being, there is Brahma. This supreme spirit is the "True Self," the *atman*. The key phrase in the Upanishads is "You Are That One"; in Sanskrit, this phrase is *Tat tvam asi*.

With the change in how the divine is envisioned, there is also a change in practice. For example, sacrifice is irrelevant to the Infinite Spirit, which is totally self-sufficient. Instead, what one is called upon to do religiously is to work to gain direct knowledge concerning the nature of one's existence, to discover the True Self. This is accomplished by turning attention from outerworldly concerns- inward. Meditation replaces sacrifice; knowledge replaces ritual. The life of renunciation, on the other hand, is a sacrifice of the world.

GREETINGS

Like members of other religious and cultural traditions, Hindus have particular methods of greeting one another in public. When meeting a friend or when showing respect to a holy person, elder, or god, a Hindu person will join his or her hands, placing the palms together in a gesture of humility. He or she then bows before the other person and says, "Namaskar," "Namaste," or "Pranam," which means "Reverent Salutations."

Hindus believe that the Infinite Spirit, Brahman, lives within the heart of every individual. Therefore, when they join their hands, it is a symbol of the concept of the meeting of two separate persons, as the "self" meets "itself." Combined with the words *namaskar* or *namaste*, the joining of the hands in greeting is intended to impart to the person, something to the effect of "I bow to God in you; I love you and I respect you, as there is no one like you."

Source: Available online at *http://www.hindunet.org/namaste/index.htm.*

THE MAHABHARATA

Hindus continued to generate very important sacred texts after the end of the Vedic period. The Hindus call these later texts *smrti*, "that which is remembered," as distinct from the Vedas, which are *shruti*, "that which is heard," referring to the texts' early oral transmission.

The smrti texts include the *Mahabharata* and the *Ramayana*. These great epics are thrilling tales of love and war. Though set many centuries before they were written in their present form, they are repositories of the ideals of classical India (from 300 B.C. to A.D. 1200) and are treasured today.

The Mahabharata, the longest epic in the world, tells the story of two sets of stepbrothers: the Pandu brothers, led by their eldest brother, Yudhisthira, and the Kuru brothers, led by Duryodhana. When the old king becomes blind, he decides to pass the kingdom of Bharata (a name for India) to his heir. Yudhisthira is the logical choice, since he exemplifies kingly virtue, whereas Duryodhana, try as he may, simply cannot equal his stepbrother.

So Duryodhana decides to win the succession with a trick. Knowing that Yudhisthira, though very righteous, has a weakness for gambling, Duryodhana brings in a cheat who is able to trick Yudhisthira out of his fortune and eventually out of his right to the succession. Yudhisthira is forced to agree that he and his brothers, the simpleminded but stouthearted Bhima and the handsome warrior Arjuna, will go into exile for twelve years. During the thirteenth year, they must disguise and hide themselves so as not to be identified. If they are found, they will forfeit the right to rule forever.

During the Pandu brothers' exile, they have many adventures. Arjuna also wins the hand of the beautiful Draupadi for his brother Yudhisthira, even though her heart belongs to Arjuna. Meanwhile, Duryodhana rules the kingdom. Despite his most ardent efforts, however, he is unable to maintain the land's prosperity, and as he struggles to improve the kingdom's fortunes, he becomes more and more oppressive in his rule.

Yudhisthira comes back to claim his right to the throne. Duryodhana arrogantly refuses even a last-minute compromise in which Yudhisthira and his brothers would be content with ruling one small city each. Civil war is inevitable.

Both sides look for allies. Both Yudhisthira and Duryodhana go to one of the major warrior tribes ruled by a man named Krishna and ask for his aid. Krishna offers a very strange proposition: Each side may choose either his warriors or him. However, if they choose him, he will not fight. Duryodhana immediately chooses the warriors. The Pandus seem to be "stuck" with the nonfighting Krishna, but Arjuna asks Krishna to be his charioteer. (In these ancient battles, charioteers were expected only to drive the chariot, not to participate in battle.)

The Bhagavad Gita

The showdown occurs on the battlefield of Kurukshetra. Both sides line up in battle formation and await the signal to attack. At this point, Arjuna asks Krishna to drive him across the front lines so he can see his enemies. Immediately upon seeing them, he is heartbroken. As is the case in any civil war, among the ranks of the enemy are some of his closest friends, relatives, and teachers. Even Duryodhana, deluded and misled as he is, is not a truly evil man. Arjuna knows that this war is going to result in social chaos. He has his doubts about the wisdom of fighting this battle and confides his doubts to Krishna.

Krishna sympathizes with Arjuna's scruples but in the end tells him that he must do his duty (dharma) and fight for his brother's righteous cause. According to the view presented in the Upanishads, Krishna tells Arjuna that, in reality, the True Self (atman) neither kills nor is killed. It is eternal and unchanging. Krishna says that everything that is born must die and everything that dies is reborn. Thus, even if Arjuna kills his enemies in their present bodies, they will be reincarnated, reborn in new bodies according to their karma. Finally, Krishna tells Arjuna that, although the two of them know that Arjuna might turn from the battle for the highest moral motives, the other Pandu warriors will think him a coward and call him disgraceful names. Krishna concludes: "Die and you win heaven. Conquer and you enjoy the earth. Stand up now, Son of Kunti, and resolve to fight. Realize that pleasure and pain, gain and loss, victory and defeat, are all one and the same: then go into battle."[6]

Arjuna wants to understand these points more clearly and engages Krishna in an extended spiritual dialogue. Their conversation reaches its climax when Arjuna realizes that he is speaking with God in human form. He asks to see Krishna in his full divine splendor, a favor that Krishna grants him. This part of the story is one of the classic descriptions of a religious vision and may well be based on an actual spiritual experience.

The battle at Kurukshetra does indeed take place. The Pandus emerge victorious though at considerable cost. Yudhisthira is then able to take his rightful place on the throne of India.

This section of the Mahabharata is known as the *Bhagavad Gita*, or "Song of the Blessed Lord," often simply called "the Gita." It is the most important part of the epic and circulates independently.

The dialogue between Krishna and Arjuna opens up a whole new dimension of religion in Hinduism. Krishna presents himself as the Supreme Lord, the Highest Personal God. All other gods are merely manifestations of him in accordance with their time, place, and spiritual aptitude. Here, we are essentially seeing a type of *theism*, a worship of one god—though, true to Hindu understanding, it is not a worship that excludes other gods.

Krishna also acknowledges the Infinite Spirit explored in the Upanishads, which underlies everything and everyone; but he tells Arjuna that it is hard to come to the necessary spiritual knowledge and that not everyone has the skill, aptitude, or circumstances to live a life of renunciation. Instead, Arjuna— and, by extension, all people—can achieve the highest spiritual benefit simply by honoring and worshiping Krishna, God the Supreme Person.

Krishna also reinterprets the meaning of sacrifice. It is no longer just making offerings to the various devas, as in the polytheistic religion of the Vedas. Nor is it abandoning all worldly concerns to seek the Infinite Spirit, as in the monistic religion of the Upanishads. Rather, it is offering up one's self and all one's actions to be made holy by Krishna—a relationship with God that is closer to monotheism.

The Bhagavad Gita is sometimes called "the Bible of popular Hinduism," and it is treasured by Hindus much as the Gospels are valued by Christians. Many Hindus memorize it and quote from it extensively to support doctrinal positions. There are devotees of Krishna, among whom are the members of the International Society of Krishna Consciousness (ISKCON), more popularly known as the Hare Krishnas, who maintain that knowledge and practice of the Gita alone will bring about salvation. The Bhagavad Gita is considered one of the world's great spiritual classics.

THE RAMAYANA

The other Hindu epic is the *Ramayana*. Like the Mahabharata, it tells the story of a prince who is sent into exile. This time, the prince is named Rama, and he is forced to leave his capital city with his beautiful wife, Sita. The demon king, Ravana, sees Sita and, lusting after her, kidnaps her and takes her to his fortress on Sri Lanka, the large island off the southeastern coast of India. Rama searches for his wife and is able to locate her with the aid of the monkey king, Hanuman, who has his monkeys form a bridge across the sea to Sri Lanka. Rama, his brother, and their army are able to cross and lay siege to Ravana's fortress. Eventually, Rama and Ravana engage in one-on-one combat and Ravana is killed. Rama is then reunited with his wife.

Sita maintains that she never yielded to Ravana, and Rama, of course, believes her. But when he returns to his kingdom, which now welcomes him, there are many who doubt Sita's virtue. She had been the prisoner of Ravana for a year, and, for all his demonic attributes, Ravana was actually a handsome man who would have been attractive to many women. To prove her virtue, Sita throws herself on a fire and remains unscathed. This act shames her accusers. Afterward, Rama and Sita reign happily. Sita becomes the model of heroic womanhood. In Hindu belief, a man is heroic in terms of his physical strength, while a woman is heroic in terms of her virtue.

These epics become the embodiment of the finest ideals in Hinduism: Rama, the brave hero determined to win back the woman he loves from a lustful demon; Yudhisthira, the righteous king even with his tragic flaw of gambling; Arjuna, the conscience-stricken warrior for right; Sita, the loving and ever-faithful wife; and Draupadi, the beautiful inspiration of heroes—all tap into universal virtues that are admired all over the world.

Modern India is determined to preserve its epic heritage, and so every means of contemporary and popular culture is used to bring these epics to life for its present-day population. Students in school read simplified stories in their textbooks based on the epics. Children of all ages find epic heroes in comic books sold at every Indian newsstand. Television programs that serialize the Ramayana have far outdistanced in popularity any competition from Western television. So fascinated are the people that once, when a television episode was delayed because of mechanical failure, there were riots in the street.

The Indian people love movies as well, and the Indian film industry is very large and active. Episodes from the epics have been the basis for innumerable movies, and a number of Indian actors and actresses specialize in portraying figures from the epics. Bombay, the center of Indian filmmaking—affectionately called "Bollywood" ("Bombay" + "Hollywood")—is one of the largest movie production systems in the world.

DEVOTIONAL LITERATURE

Theistic Hindus (those who are devotees of one of the great gods or the Goddess) generated extensive devotional literature. The eighteen great *Puranas* ("ancient texts") contain India's great mythic stories about Hinduism's many gods and goddesses. The *Agamas*, another set of popular devotional writings, are divided

PURANAS

The Puranas, which probably achieved their current form around A.D. 500, are considered perhaps the richest collection of mythology in the world. Before they were finalized in their written form, they were passed on orally, since as far back as about 1500 B.C.

There are eighteen major Puranas. Each of these long books contains different stories about the Hindu gods and goddesses, along with hymns, rules of life, details of rituals, and information about Indian history.

The most influential of the Puranas are the Shiva Purana, the Vishnu Purana, and the Markendeya Purana, which is dedicated to the Goddess. Krishna worshipers are particularly devoted to the Bhagavata Purana.

The Puranas are some of the most often used scriptural texts within the Hindu tradition. Because their encyclopedic format covers so many topics, they serve almost as guide books for all of life and society.

Source: Available online at *http://www.hindunet.org/puranas/index.htm.*

into three sections—one devoted to Vishnu, a second to Shiva, and the third to Devi. The Agamas contain theology and instructions for worship. The *Tantras* describe Shiva's conversations with his divine consort, who is the embodiment of feminine power, or "Shakti." They also describe secret spiritual practices.

The preceding survey of Hindu scriptures, as extensive as it is, does not exhaust the various types of sacred literature found in Hinduism. There are popular collections of devotional poetry associated with great poets like Tulsidas or Caitanya, and religious songs as well. Great gurus or teachers will write or dictate texts that serve as a type of scripture for their followers.

4

Worldview
of Hinduism

In his love the Lord punishes,
that the sinner may mend his
ways and follow the right.
All his acts flow from his love.

—Śivañānasiddhivar, ii. 15.

We have seen that there is no one creed or idea of divinity that defines Hinduism. The Vedas are no exception to the general rule that scriptures can be variously interpreted. The ancient Vedic Samhitas such as the Rig Veda were polytheistic. Theirs was a religion of many gods (devas), worshiped by means of sacrificial offerings. Polytheism is still an important component of Hinduism, and, although there are very few animal sacrifices, offering gifts to the gods remains central to Hindu religious practice. The Upanishads taught that behind the many gods is the Infinite Spirit, Brahman; this is the religion of monism. Here the aim of life is to discover through meditation one's true spiritual nature, which is not different from Eternal Being. In the Bhagavad Gita we see the development of the idea of a personal Supreme God. This God, though paramount in the heart of the devotee, does not preclude the existence or worship of other gods. We have called this last concept simply "theism," to distinguish it from Western monotheism.

As we have said, Hinduism is structured diversity. Hinduism finds a way to accommodate diversity while maintaining an overall structure that fits everything together.

Despite all its diversity, it is possible to discern a set of religious viewpoints and attitudes that can be labeled distinctively Hindu. We will begin this chapter with these common elements. We will look first at the human condition as Hinduism sees it: What is a human being? What is the significance of our actions (karma)? And, what are the aspirations of human life, and how can people attain their goals? This first set of inquiries constitutes what we might call Hindu "anthropology."

Next we will consider three different perspectives on the Divine, namely, polytheism, monism, and theism. Polytheism is the worship of many deities. Monism is the belief in a "One" that lies behind the many gods, persons, and things that make up the cosmos which we experience. Theism, as we are using the term, refers to an intense (but not exclusive) devotion to one of Hinduism's major deities. Our discussions of polytheism, monism, and theism will provide an overview of Hindu theology.

Finally, we will turn our attention to Hinduism's prescription for uniting the human being with the Divine. There are three main ways to accomplish this, and each is called a "yoga." We will consider, in turn, Karma Yoga (the Way of Works), Jnana Yoga (the Way of Knowledge), and Bhakti Yoga (the Way of Devotion).

HINDU ANTHROPOLOGY: THE NATURE OF BEING HUMAN

The Human Being

In Hinduism, the human person is made up of three main components which one can envision as being similar to concentric rings on a tree, or like layers of an onion. These three components are the physical body as the outermost layer, next the *jiva* ("soul"), and finally, at the center or core of one's being, the *Atman* or True Self.

The physical body is conceived, matures, grows old, and dies. The soul survives death and eventually undergoes rebirth in another body. According to the doctrine of karma and reincarnation, the characteristics and circumstances of the soul in its new body depend upon the moral quality of the soul's previous lives in its former bodies. The True Self also survives death but it remains luminous and unchanged, no matter what the condition or circumstances of the soul or body. It is like a piece of gold that can be melted down, recast, reworked in a hundred different ways and yet, through it all, the essential character of the gold remains.

The Doctrine of Karma

According to *the doctrine of karma and reincarnation,* an individual is shaped by a process of moral cause and effect which extends over many lives. The results of past deeds, including those done in past lives, shape the present lifetime. The results of acts in the present shape the future, including future rebirths.

Hindus believe that meritorious deeds enable one to be reborn in heaven among the devas, or at least to be reborn in a spiritually minded family and community so that release from the round of births and deaths (moksha) can be more easily achieved. This release from the round of births and deaths constitutes the Hindu concept of salvation. Contrariwise, evil deeds may land the doer in one of the hells, or may cause him or her to take birth in unfortunate circumstances.

The doctrine of karma says that our actions have consequences: we reap what we sow. In essence, karma is simply an extension of our common sense observations. We all know that we are shaped by our past experiences in both overt and subtle ways. The Hindu doctrine of karma extends this into past and future existences.

Persons unfamiliar with Eastern religions may think that the idea of reincarnation is simply speculation designed to satisfy curiosity regarding the afterlife. But the doctrine of karma and reincarnation does much more than that. For many Hindus (and for members of other religions that believe in reincarnation, e.g., Buddhism, Sikhism, and Jainism), it gives some assurance that there is indeed a long-term justice in the world.

The doctrine of karma accounts for why we are what we are. Things that happen to us are not mere accident. They are the result of past actions. Much of what Westerners attribute to heredity, environment, nurture, the subconscious, or other psychological factors, Hindus will attribute to karma. Even in the West, popular literary and movie plots often explore how a person's life is shaped by some one thing which they have done, whether that action be good or ill. From a Hindu perspective, these plots are case histories of the working of karma.

The doctrine of karma has social as well as psychological value. It tells people that they should behave in socially approved ways. By doing one's duty toward society (traditionally defined by the caste system), it says, one can accumulate merit toward a better future life. What strikes most Americans as unfair about the caste system is that it seems to penalize people for "accident of birth," a phrase often heard in contemporary social theory. However, if the doctrine of karma and reincarnation is correct, no birth is accidental. Every birth is the result of previous deeds.

Consequently, there is no injustice in being born in a lower caste. One should do one's duty, act virtuously, and live in the awareness that one is playing a role, performing a function, in a structure and pattern much larger than self and even society at any given historical moment.

The doctrine of karma answers seemingly unanswerable questions: Why do the virtuous suffer? Why do bad things happen to good people? Given the perspective of one lifetime, such suffering might appear meaningless, but given the perspective of many lifetimes, the virtuous may be suffering for deeds done in previous lifetimes. But is present virtue of no avail? Quite the contrary! The virtuous will be rewarded, perhaps in their present lifetime, but if not, then in a future lifetime. The wicked who prosper in this life are living off karmic capital from previous virtue. Their time will come, if not in this life, then in later lives. Many take comfort in this idea. The doctrine of karma assures them that there is justice in the world.

Human Aspirations

Life on this earth allows human beings to work toward many different goals. Hindus categorize human aspirations by recognizing four main goals for which one can live: pleasure, profit, duty, and moksha.

The first goal for which one might live is *kama* (pleasure). Kama is the enjoyment of anything which can be experienced through the senses. As in the West, "pleasure" often carries the connotation of sexual desire, but it is certainly not limited to that. It includes aesthetic appreciation, eating fine food, or rejoicing in anything associated with good living. The kind of pleasure which one pursues is related to one's karma.

Hindus believe there is nothing wrong with pleasure in its proper place, but one must also recognize its limitations. A pleasurable lifestyle is not possible for everyone. Perhaps one does not have the resources to maintain it. Even if one has sufficient resources, one may not always be in circumstances where pleasure is accessible. One must recognize as well that the life of pleasure can in itself have unpleasant consequences. One can overdo pleasures and cause harm to oneself. Repetition of pleasurable experiences can also lead to becoming "sick of" what once gave pleasure. Eventually, people recognize that pleasure is too fleeting, too short-lived, too capricious, to pin one's hopes for happiness on it. One realizes that there is more to life than indulgence, attractive as that may have seemed at one point. One then proceeds to the second goal, profit.

The next goal is *artha*, which includes both wealth and status. Once again, one's karma influences what kinds of possessions one seeks, or what kind of recognition one desires.

The pursuit of wealth, power, and fame is very natural. If done ethically and within appropriate bounds, it can lead to positive results. But in this impermanent world, what one acquires, even in honest enterprise, can be taken away in the course of events. Fame, too, is fleeting. Success and failure both depend on circumstances which may be beyond one's control. Eventually, people recognize that even if they are successful in their quest for wealth and fame, it does not bring a secure and lasting happiness. Once again, one is forced to look further.

The third goal of life is *dharma* (duty). "Duty" or "virtue" is the highest of worldly aims. If everyone lived in pursuit of the third goal, we would have a better and safer world. Nonetheless, dharma does not constitute the final goal of life because it, too, is subject to the vicissitudes of temporality. Even if one fed the entire world today, they will all be hungry again tomorrow. Even if one heals a sick person, or comforts a mourner right now, those persons will fall ill or grieve again in the future. Ultimately, one must recognize that this world is not designed to support the lasting happiness that we all crave.

All humanity recognizes that we live in a world that is constantly changing. There is no escaping this change while living here—the seasons shift, we grow older, things wear out, loved ones die. Hinduism puts this recognition in the center of its worldview. It reiterates that the world is not only impermanent, but it is also a source of disappointment. We cannot rely on it to provide our true happiness. Even if I get what I want, my desires may change because my internal world is not permanent. Or, even if I get what I want, I may as quickly lose it, because the external world is not permanent either. There are no guarantees in this world, no promises that I can get what I want, nor that what I wanted will make me happy when I get it, nor that I can keep anything that I currently have and love.

Virtually everything in the Hindu worldview flows from the awareness that all things change, both internally and externally, while what we truly desire is that our happiness should be permanent. Only the unchanging can secure our happiness. Everything else is "here today, gone tomorrow."

HINDU THEOLOGY: PERSPECTIVES ON THE DIVINE
As we have seen, Hinduism includes elements of polytheism, monism, and worship of a personal Supreme God (theism). We will examine each of these perspectives on the Divine in turn.

Polytheistic Religion: The Realms of the Devas
Right "above" us in the Hindu cosmos are the *devas* (gods) of the ancient Vedas, and, in addition, all the gods developed in 2,500 years of popular Hinduism. While these gods are much more powerful than human beings, live incredibly longer lives, and know so much more than people do, they are not God as Westerners generally understand the term. They are divine but they are not supreme. Because they are active forces in the world, sometimes associated with various natural phenomena, one must deal with them respectfully.

It is often said that there are 330 million gods in Hinduism. Nobody has actually counted them, and this number is surely an exaggeration. Nonetheless, the thrust of this statement is accurate: Hinduism's divine beings are everywhere. In truth, if one were to count all the minor spirits of only local importance as well as the major deities, one could come up with a thousand gods and goddesses at least. This is polytheistic Hinduism.

These gods and goddesses are not all equal by any means. Some of them are very minor and play a role only in small communities or villages. Others are more important and are worshiped in a larger area. The most significant would be acknowledged and honored throughout India.

The devas are continually being challenged by demonic beings called *asuras*. The devas are generally able to keep the asuras at bay, but more than occasionally an asura arises whose power is beyond that of the devas, forcing them to seek the help of higher divine beings.

Surprisingly, devas and asuras sometimes cooperate to accomplish some divine purpose. One of the most famous Hindu myths tells of the "churning of the ocean of milk." There was once a great ocean of milk which, if churned, would produce many blessings, the chief of which was Amrita, the potion of immortality. In order to churn the ocean of milk, the devas and asuras used Vishnu's serpent, Shesha, as a churning rope. The devas held on to the head, and the asuras held on to the tail. Back and forth they tugged and pulled, and the various blessings came forth, including the potion of immortality.

The most important of the devas, such as Indra and Varuna, are said to have their own heavenly palaces, where men and women with good karma reside for thousands of years between human lifetimes. Dwellers in these heavenly residences enjoy a wonderful lifestyle reminiscent of the South Sea Islands. Everything that one could ever desire grows on trees. Here one finds the most delicious food, the most beautiful of clothes and houses, and the most delightful of heavenly attendants, eager to please. The females attendants are called *apsaras*. They are portrayed as slender-waisted young women with voluptuous figures. Their male counterparts are the *gandharvas*, tall well-muscled "beach-boy" types who play guitar-like instruments and serenade guests.

The virtuous are thus rewarded with an enjoyable afterlife. All one has to do to win thousands of years of residence in these realms is to perform good deeds, and to carry out one's various household and social duties. What could possibly be wrong with such a destiny?

Living a life of pleasure for ten thousand years is most enjoyable—until one's ten thousand years is up. These heavenly realms of the devas, indeed, the devas themselves, are in the final analysis impermanent. Even Indra and Varuna, not to mention the rest, will pass away only to be reborn in other states of existence, and so also will be the fate of all who dwell within their realms.

There are hellish counterparts to the heavenly realms. Those who have done wicked deeds will be reborn in realms as horrible and painful as the heavens are pleasurable. There souls suffer extremes of heat and cold, and the pain of burning and cutting. This also may go on for a thousand years but, in the end, the hells are as impermanent as the heavens. There is no eternal damnation in Hinduism.

There is one more set of inhabitants in these spiritual realms. Yogins can acquire extraordinary powers and psychic abilities through their practice of the yogas. Highly developed yogins may ascend to various divine realms where they become godlike. However, becoming godlike is not the same as moksha or liberation, because, while the godlike status may persist for long periods of time, it is ultimately temporary. Liberation or moksha, on the other hand, is permanent.

Monistic Religion: The Search for Ultimate Reality

The wise men and women of the Upanishads sought the one Reality behind the many different things and being around us. They settled on Brahman, "Infinite Spirit," as that one, ultimate Reality.

Ultimate Reality, which is not a being but rather the basis for all being, is beyond all human categories and understanding. Nonetheless, Hindus cite "being," "consciousness," and "bliss" as attributes which at least point toward the experience of Infinite Spirit. Infinite Spirit is "being" because every individual thing in the world derives its existence from Infinite Spirit. Infinite

Spirit is not the lowest common denominator of matter, but rather it is the highest attribute found in the universe, namely, consciousness. Finally, Infinite Spirit is "bliss" because it is

WAR BETWEEN THE GODS AND THE ASURAS

The Karna Parva of the Mahabharata contains an account of a war that took place between the gods and the asuras, somewhat similar to the Greek mythological story of the battle between the Titans and the Olympians. Ultimately, the gods—not the asuras—were the victors:

Duryodhana said, —"Listen, once more, O ruler of the Madras, to what I will say unto thee, about what happened, O lord, in the battle between the gods and the Asuras in the days of yore! The great Rishi Markandeya narrated it to my sire. I will now recite it without leaving out anything, O best of royal sages! Listen to that account confidingly and without mistrusting it at all. Between the gods and the Asuras, each desirous of vanquishing the other, there happened a great battle, O king, which had Takara for its evil (root). . . . Those Asuras then, filled with joy at having obtained those boons and having settled it among themselves about the construction of the three cities [Tripura], selected for the purpose the great Asura Maya, the celestial artificer, knowing no fatigue or decay, and worshipped by all the Daityas and Danavas. Then Maya, of great intelligence, by the aid of his own ascetic merit, constructed the three cities . . . all in such a way as to revolve in a circle, O lord of Earth! Each of those cities measured a hundred Yojanas in breadth and a hundred in length. And they consisted of houses and mansions and lofty walls and porches. And though teeming with lordly palaces close to each other yet the streets were wide and spacious. And they were adorned with diverse mansions and gate-ways. . . ."

Those three Daitya kings, soon assailing the three worlds with their energy, continued to dwell and reign, and began to say,—"Who is he called the Creator?" . . . Crowned with success by means of austere penances, those enhancers of the fears of the gods sustained, O king, no diminution [sic] in battle. Stupified then by covetousness and folly, and deprived of their senses, all of them began to shamelessly exterminate the cities and towns established all over the universe. Filled with pride . . . the wicked Danavas ceased to show any respect for anybody. . . .

Duryodhana said . . . "Slay the Danavas, O wielder of the trident! O giver of honours, let the universe, through thy grace, obtain happiness. O Lord of all the worlds, thou art the one whose shelter should be sought! We all seek thy shelter."

suffused with a peaceful joy that exceeds all worldly forms of human happiness.

The Upanishads are known as the Vedanta, the "end of the

The gods said,—"Gathering all forms that may be found in the three worlds and taking portions of each, we will, O Lord of the gods, construct a car [*vimana*] of great energy for thee" . . . the Mind became the ground upon which that car stood, and Speech the tracks upon which it was to proceed. . . . With lightning and Indra's bow attached to it, that blazing car gave fierce light.

Thus equipt, that car shone brilliantly like a blazing fire in the midst of the priests officiating at a sacrifice. Beholding that car properly equipt, the gods became filled with wonder. Seeing the energies of the entire universe united together in one place, O sire, the gods wondered, and at last represented unto that illustrious Deity that the car was ready.

Then Mahadeva, terrifying the very gods, and making the very Earth tremble, ascended that car resolutely. . . . Then that Lord of the gods proceeded surrounded by all the gods, upon that large car. . . . When that boon-giving Lord, that dispeller of the fears of the three worlds, thus proceeded, the entire universe, all the gods, O best of men, became exceedingly gratified. . . . When the boon-giving Brahman, having ascended the car, set out for the Asuras, the Lord of the Universe, smiling the while, said,— "Excellent, Excellent! Proceed, O god, to the spot where the Daityas are!"

The triple city then appeared immediately before that god of unbearable energy, that deity of fierce and indescribable form, that warrior who was desirous of the slaying the Asuras. The illustrious deity, that Lord of the universe, then, drawing that celestial bow, sped that shaft which represented the might of the whole universe, at triple city. Upon that foremost of shafts . . . being shot, loud wails of woe were heard from those cities as they began to fall. . . . Burning those Asuras, he threw them down into the Western Ocean. Thus was triple city burnt and thus were the Danavas exterminated by Maheswara. . . .

Source: Karna Parva, Sections 33 and 34

Vedas." "Vedanta" is also the name of a very important school of Hindu philosophy. One branch of this philosophy, *Advaita Vedanta*, has been very influential in India. (Advaita Vedanta has also played a significant role in Hindu outreach to the Western nations.) It understands itself to be the correct interpretation of the Upanishads, and a continuation of the teaching of the Upanishads.

In the Upanishads (according to Advaita Vedanta), this present world is not fully real because it is continually changing. True reality is beyond change. Itself changeless, it underlies the changing phenomena of the world which we perceive. The changing phenomena of this world are mere "appearances," they are not ultimately real.

The Upanishads put it this way: Reality is like the sun and the world is like the sun's rays. The sun itself remains unchanged even as its rays vary through the course of the day. Alternatively, reality is like the ocean, and the world around us is like the waves on the ocean. Waves are turbulent and ever-changing, but beneath the waves is the ocean out of which they emerge. The depths of the ocean are the same throughout, unchanging and still.

Hindus call the world around us *maya*, which literally means "made-up things." Maya is often translated as "illusion." Like our vivid dreams, the world seems real enough while we are in it, but it has no significance for us once we "wake up."

Maya has a dual meaning. First, the world is filled with things that are "made" and "unmade." Everything comes into being and fades out of existence. Second, many of our beliefs about the world are essentially "made-up." They are like fictions. The great philosopher of Advaita Vedanta, Shankara, said that we live our ordinary lives like people who are walking along a dark road and suddenly see a dangerous snake. The people are petrified with fear until someone brings a torch and reveals that what they thought was a snake was actually only a piece of rope. Their fears arose out of their own mistaken perceptions, not out of the actual state of affairs.

Our everyday beliefs are quite different from the philosophical perspective of the Vedantin. Because the world around us is immediately present to us, we (mistakenly) take it for "reality." We are living our lives on false premises. We think that the Real is the changing circumstances of our lives. The Vedantin believes that this everyday perspective is essentially an illusion.

Ultimately, the Upanishads locate the cause of our human discontent in our ignorance of what is real. Like a person who stubbornly maintains that 2+2=5 and whose calculations therefore never come out right, we live in the stubborn belief that we can be truly satisfied if we can just adjust the things around us enough. In the end, such a strategy will not work.

Theistic Religion: Hinduism's Major Deities

As influential as monism has been, the most popular and widespread form of Hinduism is theism, the worship of a Supreme God of one's personal choice. One reason for theism's popularity is its relatively low degree of abstraction. Infinite Spirit is beyond all characteristics and attributes, yet the human mind needs to be able to focus on something specific, even in worship.

The highest Gods are considered to be the most exalted expression of the manifested cosmos. Such a God is the Supreme Divine Person, commonly given the generic name *Ishvara*, meaning "the Lord." He/She (Hinduism acknowledges both) is the personified form of the Divine Ground, the Infinite Spirit. Each of these Gods presides over a supreme paradise out of which one is never reborn.

As is typical of Hinduism, there is more than one "candidate" for the position of Supreme Divine Person. Reference is often made to the Hindu "Trinity": Brahma is the creator of the world, Vishnu is its preserver, and Shiva is the destroyer of the world. This formulation, however, does not capture the richness and complexity of popular devotionalism. The Indian populace pays Brahma little attention,[7] while both Vishnu and Shiva are quite popular. Another very popular deity, the Great Goddess, is not even mentioned in the "Hindu Trinity" formulation. The Great

(Continued on page 52)

SHANKARA'S ADVICE ON GOOD CONDUCT

Question: Oh venerated one, what should one adhere to?
Answer: The words of the guru.

Q: What is to be abandoned (not committed)?
A: That which is prohibited.

Q: Who is a guru?
A: One who having understood the Ultimate Reality, continues to strive always for the welfare of the disciple.

Q: What is proper?
A: Dharma.

Q: Who is the one who is clean/pure?
A: He who has a clean mind.

Q: What is toxic?
A: Disregarding the guru.

Q: What can be called a life?
A: That which is lived without blemish.

Q: Who is the truly awakened one?
A: The one who practices discretion.

Q: What is sleep?
A: Persistent foolishness in man.

Q: What yields happiness?
A: Friendship with the good.

Q: Who is skilled at destroying all distress?
A: The one who can sacrifice.

Q: What is death?
A: The condition of stupidity.

Q: What practice should one engage in?
A: One should engage in educating oneself, taking good medicine, and giving alms.

Q: Who is the blind one?
A: The one who does not work/perform.

Q: Who is a friend?
A: The one who saves you from incurring demerits.

Q: What is an ornament?
A: Good Conduct.

Q: What should man accumulate?
A: Knowledge, wealth, strength, good reputation, and merits.

Q: Who is the real enemy?
A: Unbridled Passion.

Q: What is dearer than life?
A: Maintenance of one's traditional dharma and association with the good.

Q: How can one be truly unafraid?
A: By proper management of relationship with people and things.

Q: Who are the wise?
A: Those who pursue the divine while alive on Earth.

Q: Who is the Guru for the whole world?
A: Shiva.

Q: From whom should knowledge be asked?
A: From Lord Shiva himself.

(Continued from page 49)

Goddess is also called "Shakti," a name which refers to the energy of the cosmos. She is Shiva's wife, Parvati. She has her own devotees who worship her (rather than any male deity) as the Supreme Divine Person.

Contemporary Hindu devotionalism flows in three main directions. There is a stream that focuses on Vishnu and his incarnations, a second stream that focuses on Shiva, and a third that centers on the Great Goddess.

The Worship of Vishnu

The most widespread and popular stream of devotion centers on the great God Vishnu. Worship of Vishnu is called Vaishnavism, and worshippers of Vishnu are called *Vaishnavites*. Many Vaishnavites show their devotion to Vishnu by drawing two vertical lines on their forehead. These lines represent the footprint of Vishnu upon them.

The name *Vishnu* means "the Pervader," the God who is everywhere. His name is found as far back as the Vedic samhitas where he was a god associated with the sun, and later with sacrifice.

Vishnu's wife is named *Lakshmi*, which means "good fortune." His animal vehicles[8] are Shesha, the seven-headed serpent, and the giant garuda bird, often described as a "man-eagle."

Vishnu is worshipped as himself, and just as commonly in the form of one of his ten *avatars* or "incarnations." Vishnu incarnates whenever the world needs help. As Krishna (a very popular avatar of Vishnu) says in the Gita: "Whenever sacred duty (Dharma) decays, and chaos prevails, then I create myself. To protect men of virtue and to destroy men who do evil and to set the standard of sacred duty, I appear in age after age."[9]

Vishnu took the form of a giant fish to save the legendary hero, Manu, from a great flood. (Manu is the Hindu version of Noah.) In the form of a giant boar, Vishnu restored dry land by diving down to the bottom of the ocean and bringing up the earth with his tusks.

Another of Vishnu's incarnations revolves around a recurrent theme in Hindu mythology—the powerful asura who is able, through the great power of his yogic meditation, to challenge the gods themselves. There once was an asura who forced the devas to grant him the following power: that he could not be killed by man, nor god, nor beast; that he could not be killed either by night nor by day; and that he could not be killed either inside or outside of his house. Armed with this power, the asura took over the world and became a tyrant.

But this demon-king had a son named Prahlada who was devoted to Vishnu. Prahlada worshipped Vishnu instead of his father. His father would torment and torture his son, but he could not get him to relinquish his faith in Vishnu.

One day Prahlada was tortured all day long, and his father said: "What kind of a god do you worship who is nowhere to be found?" Prahlada responded that Vishnu, the god who pervades everything, is everywhere. His father began contemptuously smashing the things in the room, saying, "Is Vishnu here?" or "Is Vishnu there?" At each point, Prahlada answered in the affirmative.

Finally, as the sun was going down, the dusk being neither night nor day, the demon-king walked to the door-post of his house so that he was neither inside it nor outside it, and he kicked the post, saying, "Is Vishnu in there?" At this exact moment, Vishnu in the form of a man-lion broke through the post. A man-lion is neither a beast nor a man nor a god because the man-lion was all three. The demon-king was killed, and Prahlada was released. He succeeded his father on the throne and ruled long, wisely, and well.

Prahlada's son, Bali, succeeded his father. Unfortunately, Bali was a greedy and arrogant king. He aspired to become like the devas themselves. The devas realized that if he carried out one of the most powerful Vedic sacrifices—the horse sacrifice—he would accomplish his goal of great divine power. The devas prayed to Vishnu to help them.

As King Bali was carrying out his sacrifice, a dwarf came to him and asked that he be granted a favor. Bali, who was under obligation to grant favors to his guests, told the dwarf that he could have what he wished. The dwarf said: "I would like all the land that I can encompass in three steps."

King Bali readily agreed to this request. The dwarf then revealed that he was Vishnu and transformed himself into his full divine form. Vishnu took one stride which encompassed all of the earth, and a second stride which encompassed all the heavens. The he said in a voice that resounded through the cosmos: "Where shall I take my third step?"

King Bali, who for all his faults was not a truly evil man, immediately repented of his sins and arrogance. He said: "Let your third stride be upon me!" Vishnu stepped upon Bali and pushed him down through the earth to the underworld. There Bali remains, serving as the righteous judge of the dead.

Other incarnations include a victorious warrior called Parasurama, portrayed with an axe, and the Buddha, who is sent to teach the world. At the end of the present world age, the tenth and last incarnation of Vishnu will appear as Kalki. Kalki is a great warrior of light, carrying the sword of righteousness (Dharma), and riding a great white horse. With him will come a great river from heaven. To the righteous, it will feel like a bath of warm milk. To the wicked it will feel like a surging stream of molten metal. The world will be cleansed and a great age of justice, righteousness, and peace will ensue.

The two most popular avatars of Vishnu are Rama and Krishna. We have already discussed the exploits of Rama, the warrior-hero of the Ramayana. It was the great devotional poet Tulsidas (1543–1623) who was responsible for retelling the story of the Ramayana as the deeds of Vishnu in the form of Prince Rama. Tulsidas' identification of Rama with Vishnu was so widely accepted that now *Rama* or *Ram* can be used simply to mean "God," without any specific reference to that incarnation. "Ram," meaning "God," was on the lips of Mahatma Gandhi when he died.

Krishna, we recall, was the charioteer-instructor of Arjuna in the Bhagavad Gita, which is part of the Mahabharata. This, however, is only one of his many exploits and, to the devotee of Krishna, not even the most important one. The Bhagavata Purana contains many stories about Krishna—as a mischievous child, as a youthful cowherd dallying with the *gopis* (cowgirls), and as an adult hero engaged in mortal combat with demons and monsters.

Krishna's romantic adventures with the gopis, often expressed in rather erotic terms, are the subject of much love poetry and many songs. Such amorous imagery is quite appropriate in devotional religion (*bhakti*), where the relation between God and the soul of the devotee is described as a relation between Lover and Beloved. Love of God is at the heart of devotionalism. Unlike the monistic, mystical religion of the Upanishads, where True Self and Infinite Spirit are one essential being, the theistic religion of devotion maintains a separation between the Divine and the human person, for it is in the very nature of personhood to be distinct from other persons, no matter how closely and intimately joined in love.

The Worship of Shiva

The second most prominent stream of devotion centers on Shiva.[10] His worship is called Shaivism, and his worshippers are called Shaivites. Shaivites indicate their devotion to Shiva by wearing three horizontal lines of ashes upon their foreheads.

Shiva's antecedents can be traced back to the Vedic god, Rudra, "the Howler," the god of the mysterious forests and strange, inexplicable occurrences. Over time, Rudra evolved into Shiva, whose name means "the auspicious one." "Auspicious" means "favorable, fortunate," but not everything about Shiva fits this description.

While Vishnu, as upholder of the cosmic order, is always a positive and benign figure, Shiva has a wild and unpredictable side. Shiva embodies and expresses the positive and negative polarities of the cosmos, and of life as we experience it. To his devotees, he is both God of Creation and God of Destruction, both kindly and fierce. He is the celibate Great Yogin, but his mythology also portrays him as a husband and father, and his primary symbol, the lingam, expresses his creative power.

All of Hinduism's major deities have many names, and Shiva is no exception. He is called *Mahadeva*, "Great God," "Lord of Animals" (Pashupati), or "Lord of Yogins" (Mahayogi). He is widely and affectionately known as Nataraja, "Lord of the Dance." The famous Nataraja statue shows Shiva dancing in a ring of fire. The fire symbolizes both destruction and the purifying, transformative power of fire. His left foot is raised, while his right foot crushes a demon. Two of his four arms (Hindu iconography often portrays multiple arms and faces) hold the fire of birth and death and the drum of time, while the other two gesture fearlessness and blessing. His long, matted locks swirl with the energy of the dance, but his face is calm and unperturbed, as befits one who is transcendent truth.

The wife of Shiva is *Parvati*, "the Mountain Girl." Shiva met her while he was meditating in the mountains. She is the Great Goddess. Shiva's animal vehicle is Nandin the Bull. Shiva is frequently worshipped in the form of the lingam, a small or large pillar in the shape of the male procreative organ. The lingam is not anatomically detailed, and it is not meant to incite sexual arousal in the viewer. Rather, it represents Shiva's creative power.

One of the most popular of Hinduism's deities, *Ganesha*, the elephant-headed god, is the son of Shiva. Incongruously, this large, jovial god has the tiny rat for his animal vehicle. Ganesha is the god of auspicious beginnings and the remover of obstacles. Taxi drivers in India often have his image in their cabs.

According to myth, Ganesha was a young baby who happened to peek at his mother while she was bathing. Shiva, who can be prudish at times, was scandalized that his son saw his mother naked and proceeded to cut off his head. Parvati scolded Shiva and told him to restore Ganesha's head. Unfortunately, the original head was lost, and the only available head was that of an elephant. Shiva fitted the elephant head on and Ganesha was as good as new!

The Worship of the Goddess

The third of Hinduism's main streams of devotion takes as its focus the wife of Shiva, Parvati. Parvati is only one of her many names. She is *Mahadevi*, "the Great Goddess"; *Uma*, "Light"; *Durga*, "Awe-inspiring"; and *Kali*, "the Black One" or "Goddess of Time." More than anything else, she is the Divine Mother to her devotees. Her animal vehicle is the lion. Her worshippers are called Shaktas, and she herself is Shakti, "the woman of power."

Shakti is the feminine energy of the cosmos, elevated to the stature of the supreme Goddess. Shiva, her husband, is passive and powerless without her divine energy stirring him to life. For Shaktas, the Goddess embodies all divine power, and it is she who is the destroyer of demons.

Once, it is said, there was a demon named Mahisha (the "Buffalo" demon) who gained great power through his yogic practice. He threatened to conquer not only the human world, but also the realm of the devas. The devas, unable to stop him, created the Goddess Durga. Armed with all the powers of the devas, the lithe Goddess rode forth on her huge cat to do battle with Mahisha. A famous frieze shows Mahisha retreating in the face of her confident advance. Durga cut off Mahisha's head and stomped all over him with her bare feet. Needless to say, Mahisha did not survive.

Another popular tale tells of a demon named *Rakta-bija*, "Blood-seed," who had a most peculiar power. Every time a drop of his blood was spilled, a demon just like him emerged from that drop. It seemed impossible to kill the demon without creating an army of new demons. However, Rakta-bija was defeated by the Goddess in the form of Kali. She hacked off his head. As his blood spilled out, thousands more like him sprang to life. Kali, however, was equal to the task. She drank every drop of his blood, so that none of it hit the ground. Consequently, none of the emerging demons survived.

The Worldview of Hindu Theism

If one asks, "Which of these many gods is the true God?" a Hindu is likely to be confused by the question. They will probably

answer that they are all the true God. They are all manifestations of the One Divine who reveals Him/Her/Itself in many ways
according to the inclination of the worshipper. Human beings are
different and so God is going to be different for each person.

In practice, a Hindu generally follows the worship patterns of
his or her family. Every family has a family god. If a person grows
up in a Vaishnavite family, they worship Vishnu. If one's family
is Shaivite, one honors Shiva. However, Hindus are generally
very tolerant of family members who feel drawn to worship God
in some other form than that of the family god. This is based on
the theological premise that all the gods are ultimately one. Since
family is so important, even those who worship other deities will
always do honor to the traditional god of the family.

Ramanuja (dates uncertain, perhaps ca. A.D. 1017–1137),
the great Vaishnavite theologian, is the premier philosopher
of devotional religion. Like Shankara, the great philosopher
of monistic religion, Ramanuja based his theology on the
Upanishads. Ramanuja interpreted the Upanishads in a way
quite different from Shankara, however.

For Shankara, the world is a projection from Reality rather
than having independent existence. The world is like rays from
the sun or waves on the ocean: the only unchanging and true
reality is the sun or the ocean; the rays and the waves are insubstantial and very temporary forms. Individual persons and things
are like the rays and the waves—insubstantial and temporary
forms. The only True Reality, according to Shankara, is Infinite
Spirit (Brahman). Renunciation of the world and adherence to
the path of knowledge and meditation is the only true way to
obtain release from the world. Devotional religion has its value,
but it is primarily a stepping stone to mystical religion. Moksha is
essentially being absorbed into the Infinite Consciousness just as
a drop of water is absorbed into the sea.

Ramanuja argued that both God and the world were real. If
this is so, one need not turn away from life in this world in order
to fulfill one's spiritual needs. Following the advice of the Gita,
one should carry out one's dharma without self-interest, with no

investment at all in praise or blame for one's deeds. In this view, moksha is not being absorbed into the Infinite, but rather, dwelling in a paradise with God and enjoying the divine presence forever.

The Yogas

Yoga is a cognate of the English word *yoke*. Like yoke, it can mean either "to join two things together" (as when two oxen are yoked together), or "discipline" (as when one accepts the yoke of a spiritual teaching and way of life). Yoga is a spiritual discipline used for the purpose of attaining union with either Brahman or God.

Yoga guides practitioners toward a direct awareness of truth, or an experience of the Divine. Body and mind are disciplined in order to attain higher or more profound states of consciousness.

A male who practices yoga is a *yogin* or *yogi*; a female practitioner is a *yogini*. There are a number of different forms of yoga. Which yoga one takes up depends upon one's life circumstances, and upon one's psychological traits. Hinduism recognizes that even in the area of spirituality, it is not the case that "one size fits all."

There are three primary forms of yoga. The first is the Way of Works or *Karma Yoga* (the root meaning of the word "karma" is "action" or "deed"). It involves the performance of ritual, ethical, and social duties. The second is *Jnana Yoga*, the Way of Knowledge. It involves meditation, reflection, and analysis. Its goal is recognition of the divine principle (the Atman) within oneself. The third is *Bhakti Yoga*, the Way of Devotion. It involves worship, honor, and other acts of devotion directed toward one of Hinduism's great deities.

Karma Yoga (The Way of Works)

Karma Yoga (The Way of Works) uses everyday life and everyday activities as the basis for spiritual exercises. For those who cannot spend long hours focusing the mind through meditation, it offers work as a means of focusing one's mind. In addition to the work involved in one's profession or occupation, it includes the performance of rituals and good deeds.

This yoga cultivates the ability to perform actions wholeheartedly and because they are intrinsically good, not for reward (reward is for the ego). One does one's work in the world without reference to punishment or reward. Only in such a manner can actions be purified from ego attachment.

The Way of Works includes performance of rituals and ethical behavior. In the context of Hinduism, ethical behavior means acting in accord with righteousness and performing one's *dharma* (duty) in society as defined by one's caste. At the very least, by following this path, one generates conditions for favorable rebirth, even rebirth among the devas in their heavenly realms. Some would say that even more is possible. They claim that by doing one's everyday tasks in a detached manner (without ego attachment), it is possible to win full release (*moksha*).

The Way of Works affirms both ritual and ethics. It continues the spirit of the ancient sacrificial religion of the Vedas by centering on patterned ritual behavior. It also affirms that righteousness and moral behavior are an indispensable foundation to a successful life in the world and in the afterlife.

Jnana Yoga (The Way of Knowledge)

Monistic religion finds its practical application in the Way of Knowledge (Jnana Yoga). It is a form of mysticism. A mystic is someone who has had a direct experience of ultimate reality. Having a mystical experience typically convinces a person that true reality is something completely other than what he or she thought it was, and likewise completely other than what most people continue to think it is.

For the Vedantin, the root cause of human misery is ignorance, and the final solution to our problem is knowledge (*jnana*) of a special kind. Jnana is not mere information. It is a deep, penetrating, direct insight into the nature of reality. We might call it a mystical experience.

(Continued on page 64)

THE YOGA SUTRAS OF PATANJALI

Part One:

Before beginning any spiritual text it is customary to clear the mind of all distracting thoughts, to calm the breath, and to purify the heart.

1.1. Now, instruction in Union.

1.2. Union is restraining the thought-streams natural to the mind.

1.3. Then the seer dwells in his own nature.

1.4. Otherwise he is of the same form as the thought-streams.

1.5. The thought-streams are five-fold, painful and not painful.

1.6. Right knowledge, wrong knowledge, fancy, sleep, and memory.

1.7. Right knowledge is inference, tradition, and genuine cognition.

1.8. Wrong knowledge is false, illusory, erroneous beliefs or notions.

1.9. Fancy is following after word-knowledge empty of substance.

1.10. Deep sleep is the modification of the mind which has for its substratum nothingness.

1.11. Memory is not allowing mental impressions to escape.

1.12. These thought-streams are controlled by practice and non-attachment.

1.13. Practice is the effort to secure steadiness.

1.14. This practice becomes well-grounded when continued with reverent devotion and without interruption over a long period of time.

1.15. Desirelessness towards the seen and the unseen gives the consciousness of mastery.

1.16. This is signified by an indifference to the three attributes, due to knowledge of the Indweller.

1.17. Cognitive meditation is accompanied by reasoning, discrimination, bliss, and the sense of "I am."

1.18. There is another meditation which is attained by the practice of alert mental suspension until only subtle impressions remain.

1.19. For those beings who are formless and for those beings who are merged in unitive consciousness, the world is the cause.

1.20. For others, clarity is preceded by faith, energy, memory, and equalminded contemplation.

1.21. Equalminded contemplation is nearest to those whose desire is most ardent.

1.22. There is further distinction on account of the mild, moderate, or intense means employed.

1.23. Or by surrender to God.

1.24. God is a particular yet universal indweller, untouched by afflictions, actions, impressions, and their results.

1.25. In God, the seed of omniscience is unsurpassed.

1.26. Not being conditioned by time, God is the teacher of even the ancients.

1.27. God's voice is Om.

1.28. The repetition of Om should be made with an understanding of its meaning.

1.29. From that is gained introspection and also the disappearance of obstacles.

1.30. Disease, inertia, doubt, lack of enthusiasm, laziness, sensuality, mind-wandering, missing the point, instability— these distractions of the mind are the obstacles.

1.31. Pain, despair, nervousness, and disordered inspiration and expiration are co-existent with these obstacles.

1.32. For the prevention of the obstacles, one truth should be practiced constantly.

1.33. By cultivating friendliness towards happiness and compassion towards misery, gladness towards virtue, and indifference towards vice, the mind becomes pure.

1.34. Optionally, mental equanimity may be gained by the even expulsion and retention of energy.

1.35. Or activity of the higher senses causes mental steadiness.

1.36. Or the state of sorrowless Light.

1.37. Or the mind taking as an object of concentration those who are freed of compulsion.

1.38. Or depending on the knowledge of dreams and sleep.

1.39. Or by meditation as desired.

1.40. The mastery of one in Union extends from the finest atomic particle to the greatest infinity.

1.41. When the agitations of the mind are under control, the mind becomes like a transparent crystal and has the power of becoming whatever form is presented. knower, act of knowing, or what is known.

1.42. The argumentative condition is the confused mixing of the word, its right meaning, and knowledge.

1.43. When the memory is purified and the mind shines forth as the object alone, it is called non-argumentative.

1.44. In this way the meditative and the ultra-meditative having the subtle for their objects are also described.

1.45. The province of the subtle terminates with pure matter that has no pattern or distinguishing mark.

1.46. These constitute seeded contemplations.

1.47. On attaining the purity of the ultra-meditative state there is the pure flow of spiritual consciousness.

1.48. Therein is the faculty of supreme wisdom.

1.49. The wisdom obtained in the higher states of consciousness is different from that obtained by inference and testimony as it refers to particulars.

1.50. The habitual pattern of thought stands in the way of other impressions.

1.51. With the suppression of even that through the suspension of all modifications of the mind, contemplation without seed is attained.

(Continued from page 60)

While mystical experiences can happen spontaneously, training in certain mental disciplines can help bring them about. Jnana Yoga, or the Way of Knowledge, is one of these disciplines. It emphasizes meditation and the cultivation of insight. One focuses the mind and turns one's attention inward. As the practitioner enters deeper states of awareness, he or she may directly experience the Atman, and thereby achieve union ("yoga") with Ultimate Reality.

Advaita Vedanta teaches that at the core of our being, there is the unchanging True Self, the *Atman*. Key to Vedanta is the understanding that the Atman is not different from Brahman, the Infinite Spirit and divine ground of all beings. Human destiny is to be reborn in different bodies until one achieves release from the continuous cycle of birth and death (moksha) by realizing the identity of Atman and Brahman, thereby establishing full relation with the Eternal.

Jnana Yoga, the Way of Knowledge, teaches careful discrimination between the true and the false, the real and the illusory. Knowledge here is not mere information—it is a transformation and reorientation of mind by direct insight into the nature of both the world around us and the nature of ultimate reality. It aims for a detachment from ego through three stages. The first stage is accomplished through learning and study with a guru or spiritual teacher. The second stage is accomplished on one's own, through thinking and critical reflection. The final stage is accomplished through meditation, leading to the recognition of the unity of Atman (True Self) and Brahman (Infinite Spirit).

Meditation is sometimes referred to as Raja Yoga. Classical texts define it as "ceasing the mind's turning." Raja Yoga is a combined physical and mental discipline designed to give rise to a direct experience of ultimate reality. While such "mystical" experiences can occur spontaneously, India has developed techniques to bring them about. Such techniques are found in one form or another in many Indian religious traditions, not just Hinduism.

THE FIRST LETTER FROM LORD GANESHA

Glitter, glint and gleam your temples. Clean them well.
These are the twinkle that is seen by those who do not see.
Guard the gilded throne of Siva's stall.
Keep it well lit and open.

No night doth fall upon His Holy Form.
He is the Sun, both cold and warm.

Piercing vision of deep, inner spinning wheels
pierces through the twinkle and the clinkle of your temple Ferris wheel.
These enjoy the darshan flooding out. Those caught in chain-like
discs of darker hours see only glitter and the flowers.

When we come, as puja calls, we hardly see those
who cannot see. We see those who can, clear and
crisp, their wasp-like form in the temple,
they adorn lovingly the floors.

I tell you this, Saivite brahmin souls,
have no fear to shine the sparkle all the year.
Gild the gilded forms anew so that your temples
appear just built. Appeal to every chakra wheel; one spins one and
then the other.

Gild—the base, the rudder, the anchor of it all—doth stimulate.
And sound, the one that hears. Smell, the controller of the glands.
And so, when chakras spin all through,
your temple will be always new.

Once you realize that some see, and others do not condescend to
kneel, but stand and look with open mouth as sight and sound rush
in along with drainage from the bath, be not afraid to open wide the
door. Those who enter will eventually prostrate on the floor.

Keep it clean, and gild and glint anew.
That is your job, what you have to do.

Love,
Lord Ganesha

—Vishayasuchi

The classical outline of this path is found in the *Yoga Sutras* of Patanjali, a classical Indian philosopher. He said that there are "Eight Limbs" of yoga. The first two limbs are the social and ethical foundations for practice. The first limb consists of the five vows or restraints: avoiding violence (*ahimsa*), lying, theft, sexual indulgence, and greed. The second limb consists of the five observances: purification, contentment, austerity, study, and devotion.

Next the body is prepared and disciplined through certain physical postures. This is the subject of *Hatha Yoga*, probably the best known form of yoga in the United States. This training of the body is believed to aid in disciplining the mind.

The fourth limb is control of the breath. Since breath is the source of vitality, it is believed that one can control one's inner energies by controlling one's breathing. "Following the breath" (observing one's own breathing process) is a very effective way to enter into meditation.

The fifth limb is the withdrawal of the senses. One withdraws the attention from the external world and directs it inward, refusing to grant external stimuli any influence over one's mind.

The last three limbs focus on control of the mind. The sixth limb is concentration—fixing the mind on an object of meditation and training the mind to focus exclusively on this one thing. This often involves the use of a *mantra*, a sound or series of sounds which is said to have a particular effect upon the mind when repeated or concentrated on.

The seventh limb is meditation—being able to quiet the mind and steadfastly concentrate upon the object of meditation. When one is able to do this, it empties the mind of thought.

The eighth and final limb is *samadhi*, which is a state of altered consciousness brought about by meditation. There are different levels of samadhi, the highest being moksha or release. Moksha consists of union with the Infinite Spirit.

Bhakti Yoga (The Way of Devotion)

Devotional Hinduism encourages people to relate to God in much the same way as persons relate to each other. Whereas the

Way of Knowledge leads to a recognition of the non-duality between one's True Self and Infinite Spirit, the Way of Devotion leads to increasing depths of love for a personal God.

Devotees first concentrate on loving God as they love a superior person, e.g., someone who is their lord, master, father, or mother. In the next stage of love, they relate to God as they would to a close friend. The third type of devotional love is the inverse of the first type. Whereas one began by imagining God as one's mother or father, God is now thought of as the child and the devotee becomes the parent. Like any vulnerable, helpless child, the image of the deity is wakened, fed, bathed, and put to sleep. In the final stage of love, one relates to God as one would relate to one's beloved or spouse. In this last type of love, which is the most intense form of devotion, God and soul are separate but are capable of being joined just as the souls of human lovers are knit together.

In devotional religion, one surrenders oneself to God in faith. Release is achieved less as a result of one's own exertions in meditation and more through God's act of grace. The exact role of the believer's own effort and works in the process of salvation is as extensively debated in Indian theism as it is in Christianity.

The theological division between self-effort and grace is neatly described as the difference between "monkey-hold" and "cat-hold" concepts of salvation. Some Hindus believe that moksha or liberation, while always through God's grace, may require the believer's cooperation just as a baby monkey must hold onto its mother's back as she climbs out of harm's way. For others, salvation is entirely God's work with nothing left over for the believer to accomplish. Just as the mother cat picks up the kittens by the scruff of their necks and carries them to safety with no effort on their part, so likewise does the deity carry his or her devotees to moksha.

In devotional texts and practices, the Infinite Spirit recedes in theological importance. It is far easier for something that is above the attributes of personhood to be an object of meditation

WHAT IS MEDITATION?

Many seekers work or even struggle regularly with their meditations, especially those who are just beginning. "How does one know if he is really meditating or not?" That's a question that a lot of people who meditate ask themselves. When you begin to *know,* having left the process of thinking, you are meditating at that point. When you sit down and think, you are beginning the process of meditation. For instance, if you read a metaphysical book, a deep book, and then sit quietly, breathe and start pondering what you have been reading, well, you're not quite meditating. You're in a state called concentration. You're organizing the subject matter. When you begin to realize the interrelated aspects of what you have read, when you say to yourself, "That's right. That's right," when you get these inner flashes, the process of meditation has just begun. If you sustain this intensity, insights and knowledge will come from the inside of you. You begin to connect all of the inner flashes together like a string of beads. You become just one big inner flash. You know all of these new inner things, and one insight develops into another, into another, into another. Then you move into a deeper state, called contemplation, where you feel these beautiful, blissful energies flow through the body as a result of your meditation. With disciplined control of awareness, you can go deeper and deeper into that. So, basically, meditation begins when you move out of the process of thinking. . . .

Many people use meditation to become quieter, relaxed, or more concentrated. For them, that is the goal, and if that is the goal, that is what is attained, and it's attained quite easily. However, for the deeper philosophical student the goal is different. It's the realization of the Self in this life. Meditation is the conveyance of man's individual awareness toward that realization. Each one, according to his evolution, has his own particular goal. If he works at it, he fulfills that goal. For example, a musician playing the piano might be satisfied with being able to play simple, easy tunes to entertain himself and his friends. Yet, another musician more ambitious in the fine arts might want to play Bach and Beethoven. He would really have to work hard at it. He would have to be that much more dedicated, give up that much of his emotional life, intellectual life and put that much more time into it. So it is in meditation.

—Dhyana Kala

Source: Available online at *http://www.himalayanacademy.com/books/mws/mws_ch-37.html.*

than it is for it to be an object of devotion. The lesser devas like-wise recede in importance in devotional Hinduism. The realms of the lesser devas are impermanent, and their powers insignificant next to the radiance of a supreme personal God such as Krishna or Rama, each of whom inhabits a paradise which is permanent and where the believer can enjoy the blissful Divine presence forever.

5

Hindu Worship and Temple Practice

O Servant, where dost thou seek me?
Lo! I am beside thee.
I am neither in temple nor in mosque:
I am neither in Kaaba nor in Kailash. . . .

—Trans. Rabhdranath Tagore,
One Hundred Poems of Kabīr

IMAGES OF THE DIVINE

J ewish and Muslim houses of worship are imageless. Christianity is more divided on the use of religious images, but many of its places of worship are also devoid of images. Hinduism's attitude toward religious images stands in stark contrast to this Western proclivity.

Images of the gods and goddesses are everywhere in India. One soon learns how to distinguish one deity from another by the attributes of the images. For example, Krishna is blue in color, is typically portrayed as a youth, and often plays a flute. Vishnu may have a seven-headed serpent overshadowing him. Shiva is shown holding a trident, and he may be standing by a bull. The Goddess is readily recognizable standing by her lion.

Many Hindu images have multiple arms or faces. Multiple arms symbolize the deity's powers. For example, Vishnu holds in his four hands a conch shell, a wheel, a club, and a lotus flower. Of these, the chakra, or wheel, is the most important. It is the symbol of the power by which he controls the universe. The spires of temples dedicated to Vishnu are marked with a chakra.

Shiva, the great god of destruction, is also portrayed with four arms when he dances as Nataraja. His upper right hand holds the drum of time, while the upper left hand holds a flame, symbolizing destruction. His lower hands gesture blessing and fearlessness. Although he does not hold a trident when portrayed as Nataraja, the trident is nonetheless one of Shiva's primary symbols. If the spire of a temple is marked with a trident, then that temple is dedicated to Shiva.

Hindus are well aware that no image or symbol can possibly exhaust the meaning of God. Nevertheless, the human mind needs a focus, a center of attention, a way of visualizing the invisible, of conceiving the inconceivable. These images make the gods of Hinduism seem more present and real.

Temple images may be unmoving or moving. The unmoving images are large and made of stone. The moving images are typically made of an alloy of metals. Moving images are taken out in procession on festival days.

THE DESIGN OF A TEMPLE

Much of Hindu religious practice is carried out at home shrines, but temples are very important as well. There are thousands of temples in India ranging in size from large complexes that can accommodate several hundred worshipers to small village shrines. Some of the temples date back a thousand years and have a long and venerable history associated with them. There are also new temples being built both in India and in Hindu communities all over the world. Often, a wealthy industrialist or entrepreneur will sponsor the building of a new temple or the renovation of an old one as a means of showing devotion and as a form of community service.

A temple is designed to reflect the entire universe. Its floor plan is a symbolic, miniature representation of the cosmos. The floor plan is a grid of squares and equilateral triangles. The square is a mystical form in Hinduism. The grid, which is in fact a mandala, a model of the cosmos, typically contains 64 or 81 squares, with each square belonging to a deity. The square in the center represents the deity to whom the temple is dedicated.

The entrance to the main shrine should face east, toward the rising sun. Worshipers begin at the entryway and move through a series of increasingly sacred spaces, until they reach the *garbagriha* (literally, "womb chamber"), which is the "holy of holies" of a Hindu temple. The tower or spire of a Hindu temple is erected directly above the garbagriha.

Temples are generally placed near shade and water, since the Puranas state that "The gods always play where groves are near rivers, mountains and springs." The gods like mountains as well, so temples have soaring towers that look like mountains. At one time, temples were painted white to make them look even more like snow-covered mountains.

Many ancient peoples thought of caves as sacred places, and India was no exception. The earliest Buddhist, Jain, and Hindu shrines are rock-cut caves. In Hindu temples, the garbagriha is designed to resemble a cave. It is small and dark. Even though numerous sculptures dance across the external walls of temples, the massive walls of the garbagriha are unadorned. The visitor moves from the bright light of day outside the temple to the darkness of the inner sanctuary, from a profusion of visual forms on the external walls to the visual simplicity of the garbagriha.

THE TEMPLE OF THE SUN GOD AT KONARK

Many of India's grand temples are in a state of ruin or disrepair. Weather, invaders, and merely the passage of centuries have all taken their toll. Even ruined temples, however, can continue to attract large numbers of pilgrims and tourists. The Temple of Surya (the Sun God), located in Konark in the state of Orissa, provides one example.

The Konark Sun Temple was built in 1278 by a medieval Indian king, Narasimha Deva. Its ruins were unearthed in the late nineteenth century. Only the assembly hall is fully intact. The tower over the garbagriha is missing, and many fragments have fallen out of their original position. However, it is awe-inspiring even in its present state. India has issued a postage stamp featuring the Sun Temple at Konark, and UNESCO has declared it a world heritage site.

The entire temple replicates in stone the chariot in which Surya, the Sun God, is said to ride through the sky every day. The base of the temple is an immense platform with twelve sculpted wheels on each side. Each wheel is ten feet high. The temple building was erected on this platform. The platform plus the temple building constituted Surya's carriage. This carriage was drawn by seven magnificently carved horses, all straining together to pull it.

The immense scale of the temple's architecture is balanced by its exquisite sculptures. The entire exterior of the temple (base, walls, and roof) is covered with sculpted stone images of animals, foliage, and people. There are also freestanding sculptures, including three images of Surya positioned to catch the sun's rays at dawn, noon, and sunset. Hindu sculpture is lithe and fluid, creating the impression that even the stone figures might at any moment come down off their walls and pedestals and dance away. Consequently, the stone images of kings and queens, dancers, musicians, animals, and mythical beasts create a vibrant panorama of all of life quickened by the sun.

TEMPLE ECONOMICS

A millennium ago, temples were maintained through donations from royalty and other wealthy patrons, who gave the temples gold, silver, livestock, and grants of land. Donors were believed to receive religious merit in return, shortening their journey toward liberation (moksha).

Some temples became very wealthy. They hired priests and suppliers of garlands, ghee (clarified butter), milk, oil, rice, fruits, sandalwood paste, and incense. A detailed account of those supported by Rajarajeshwara Temple at Tanjore in A.D. 1011 listed six hundred people. They included dancing girls, singers, drummers, conch-blowers, accountants, parasol bearers, potters, carpenters, astrologers, and tailors. In return for their work at the temple, these people were given land to cultivate so they could make a living. By providing livelihoods for such large numbers of people, the temple exercised enormous influence on the economic life of the community.

TEMPLE GUARDIANS KEEP OUT DEMONS, WELCOME VISITORS

The entrances to Hindu and Jain temples in India are protected by guardians or gatekeepers (*Dwarapakalas*). These are not real persons, but painted or sculpted figures. Often the guardians are depicted as strong, male devotees, because their job is to keep out demons and undesirable influences. However, some temple entrances are guarded by female figures, or by male figures that are not exceptionally muscular.

Hanuman (the monkey-king of the Ramayana) and the Garuda bird (Vishnu's animal vehicle) are the most common guardians of Hindu temples. The guardians of the Narayani temple in Kumta are the sun and the moon. Popular personalities and entertainers may also be pressed into service as temple guardians. In a temple in Honavar, celestial women playing musical instruments guard the entrance.

The guardians serve as greeters as well as "bouncers." Perhaps because they are a visitor's first impression, temple artists and architects appear to have expended considerable efforts in their creation.

Hindus today continue to donate vast sums of money to temples. For example, the Vishnu temple at Tirumala has an annual income of around $165 million, much of which it expends in charity. This temple has a staff of six thousand persons and receives approximately thirty thousand pilgrims per day.

INSIDE THE TEMPLE COMPLEX

There may be yearly, monthly, weekly, or daily rounds of services, depending upon the temple and the deities housed in it. The temples are generally open to believers all day so that they can come, make offerings, pray, and listen to religious teachers who may make a particular temple the center of their activities. Some temples are open to anyone who cares to visit, while others restrict entrance to Hindus.

The major temples are not just a single building, but rather an entire area, usually surrounded by a small wall. Inside the wall are smaller buildings and shrines as well as the main worship hall. Various gods and goddesses are installed in different sections of the temple. Typically, the minor shrines will contain deities associated with the main deity. In a temple dedicated to Vishnu, auxiliary deities may include Lakshmi (Vishnu's wife), Garuda (his animal vehicle), Sita (Rama's wife; Rama is an incarnation or avatar of Vishnu), or Hanuman (the monkey hero of the Ramayana). Auxiliary shrines in a temple dedicated to Shiva may house Parvati (Shiva's wife), Ganesha, or Karttikeya (Shiva's sons).

Trees are planted within the temple complex. India is a tropical country, and the weather is sometimes oppressive, so it is not surprising that trees offering cool shade and shelter from the rain are considered sacred. In both ancient and modern India, shrines tend to be situated under trees. Even today, it is not unusual to see small offerings placed under large trees in forests and parks.

Most temples have a *parikrama*, a broad circular path around the shrine area. Pilgrims use this path to "circumambulate"

The Kumbha Melas are a unique kind of pilgrimage. They are bathing festivals that occur four times every twelve years, once at each of the following four locations: Prayag, Haridwar, Ujjain, and Nasik. A Kumbha Mela takes place when the planet Jupiter enters Aquarius and the Sun enters Aries. Once in every twelve-year cycle, the Maha ("great") Kumbha Mela takes place at Prayag, where three holy rivers (the Ganga, the Yamuna, and the Saraswati) converge. Millions of people participate in the Maha Kumbha Mela, making it one of the largest gatherings of pilgrims in the world, numerically in the same league as the Hajj (the Muslim pilgrimage to Mecca), although the latter is an annual event, whereas the Maha Kumbha Mela only occurs once every twelve years.

WORSHIP IN HOMES

Worship occurs in homes as well as in temples. Every Hindu home has a shrine in some part of the house, usually tucked away in a private section. Here, the god or gods of the family are given puja and worshiped. They are treated as the family would treat an honored guest: They are bathed, fed, dressed, and presented with offerings of flowers and incense. All of this may strike Westerners as rather quaint, since the Western conception of God is that of a being who is above all human necessities, such as eating and sleeping. Hindus believe this just as their Western counterparts do. But the essential message here is that human beings should relate to the gods in the same way that people relate to other people. One approaches the deity as if the deity were one's king, parent, judge, lover, or friend. And just as people "go all out" to honor their parents and friends, so should they do the same for their divine guests. Treating the deity just as one treats those human beings one loves signifies that the deities are never distant or remote. Human beings are continually in their presence.

Altar furnishings are dependent upon one's devotional

tradition. Vaishnavites will often have a *tulasi* (basil) plant, since it is sacred to Vishnu. They may also have smooth black stones called *shalagramas* on the altar. Shaivites may display the lingam or small models of the bull Nandin.

6

Growing Up Hindu

So like a happy child I play
In Thy dear world, O God.

—Nicol Manicol, *Psalms of Marāthā Saints,*

THE SAMSKARAS

Traditional Hinduism offers rituals for every stage of a person's life, from conception to death. These life cycle rituals are called *samskaras*, and there can be as many as twenty-one of them. Although most contemporary Hindus do not take part in all of them, they remain socially significant markers of the process of growing up as a Hindu.

Many of these rituals cluster in the earliest years of a child: rites of conception, of protection of a fetus, of birth, of taking a baby outdoors to see the sun for the first time, and so forth. Perhaps the most significant ritual for a young man is the *upanayana* ceremony, which marks his passage to adulthood. Just as people of other religions often prefer a religious marriage service to a secular one, so do many Hindus. The Hindu marriage ceremony is rather lengthy, taking several days to complete. Funeral rites mark the end of an individual lifetime. The purpose of these various rituals is to smooth the transition from one stage of life to the next, and to pray for blessings for the person or persons undergoing the ceremony.

GENDER ROLES

Hindu society is diverse, but the majority of the populace remains traditional in outlook and values. Traditional societies in general, whether in India or elsewhere, tend to maintain a stricter differentiation between gender roles. Therefore, the process of growing up Hindu is different for boys than it is for girls.

The traditional Hindu family still desires sons, as do traditional families in most parts of the world. The reasons for this are simple: It is the sons who carry on the family name and who labor as adults to maintain the family property, eventually

CHILDREN AND PARENTS

Children should follow in their parents' footsteps and having become like them, serve them to the best of their ability.

—Atharva Veda

inheriting those holdings. Daughters lose their family name when they are married, and they generally go to live with their husband's family. Therefore, a daughter's adult labor benefits her husband's family, not her family of origin. No matter how many children she gives birth to, they will not inherit her family name, nor can she inherit her father's property.

The work of the United Nations (UN) and other global organizations has led to a general improvement of attitudes toward women in traditional societies. It is important to remember as well that the vast majority of Hindu families have always loved their daughters dearly, despite the economic burden involved in raising them. It was traditional family patterns, not the families themselves, that disadvantaged daughters.

Family is very important in Hinduism. The general social pattern even today is the "extended family." Where there is an extended family pattern, relatives usually live within a short distance of each other and have an on-going interaction with each other. In contrast to the "nuclear family" of the United States, which consists only of father, mother, and dependent children, an extended family includes grandparents, adult sons and their families, and perhaps other relatives as well. In the United States, adult children are expected to establish independent households, often at some distance from their parents' homes. More distant relatives are often more distant in location as well, and there may not be much interaction with them. Although many Hindus in the United States appreciate being in "the land of opportunity," they are often critical of the state of the family and family values in the United States. Of course, since traditional families tend to disadvantage women, this criticism is directly and inversely related to criticism of the treatment of women in India. It seems that no society has yet found a way to have both gender equality and strong extended families.

THE FOUR STAGES OF LIFE

The Hindu tradition divides a human lifetime into four stages. Although there are many samskaras associated with infancy and

B

The mysterious Hindu god Shiva represents the conflicting forces within the cosmos: He is both gentle and fierce, destructive and creative. Seen here enthroned upon his traditional vehicle, the bull, he holds on his lap his wife, Parvati. As the wife of Shiva, Parvati (who, like Shiva, has many different names) is the focus of a separate Hindu tradition of worship—the worship of the Goddess. In her role as the supreme Goddess, Parvati takes on the dominant role and Shiva becomes the more passive partner. This painting of the divine couple, housed in the Victoria and Albert Museum in London, was done around 1780 in the Eastern Deccan Plateau region of India.

This is a page from the "Nirvanaprakarama" or "Exposition of Greeting," a Hindu text that provides information about the practice of yoga. Housed in the collection of the Musée Condé in Chantilly, France, this ornately designed leaf is written in Sanskrit, using the Devanagari script first developed around the twelfth century A.D.

Built in the ninth century, Borobudur Temple in Java, Indonesia (seen here in an aerial shot), was a Hindu and Buddhist temple that had a major influence on the architectural style of later temples. Although the temple was abandoned sometime in the eleventh century, it was excavated during the twentieth century and made a national monument in Indonesia.

Ganesha, whose statue is seen here decorated with hibiscus flowers, is one of the most popular gods in the Hindu pantheon. Ganesha is the god of new beginnings and of overcoming obstacles. Images of Ganesha almost always have at least four hands and sometimes many more. Each hand carries a separate symbolic object. Ganesha is frequently shown with one hand outstretched in a gesture of protection, and the second hand holding a sweet (*modaka*), to symbolize the sweetness of self-realization. In the other two hands, he often holds an elephant goad and a noose. The goad is used to prod a person along on the path of truth, while the noose (which symbolizes worldly desires) reminds viewers that strong attachments to the world serve as a severe restraint—like a noose—on a soul.

This seventeenth-century painting depicts "The Hour of Cowdust," a famous episode recounted in the Bhagavata-Purana. Housed in the National Museum at New Delhi, this work depicts large numbers of cows (which, of course, are held sacred by Hindus) being led to safety, in preparation for an approaching thunderstorm.

This miniature painting depicts Vishnu, the preserver god, riding on the back of his vehicle, Garuda, the swift-flying bird, who, according to legend, helps Lord Vishnu spread knowledge of the Vedas and feelings of courage among the faithful. Riding with Vishnu is his wife, Devi Lakshmi, the goddess of wealth.

This painting from the seventeenth-century Mewar School depicts a popular tale about the god Krishna. According to legend, Krishna convinced the shepherds to worship cows and the Govardhan Mountain. As part of their worship, they performed the Giri Yadnya ritual instead of their usual worship of the god Indra. As a result, Indra became angry and ordered a cloud to pour heavy rains on the people. The damaging rains caused floods and forced cows to flee in search of shelter. Krishna was furious. To stop the rains, he lifted up the Govardhan Mountain and held it in mid-air, creating an enormous umbrella. The shelter it provided allowed the people to bring their possessions and cows to safety. Seeing this, Indra realized he could not defeat Krishna and allowed the clouds to retreat. Krishna was then able to restore the mountain to its proper home.

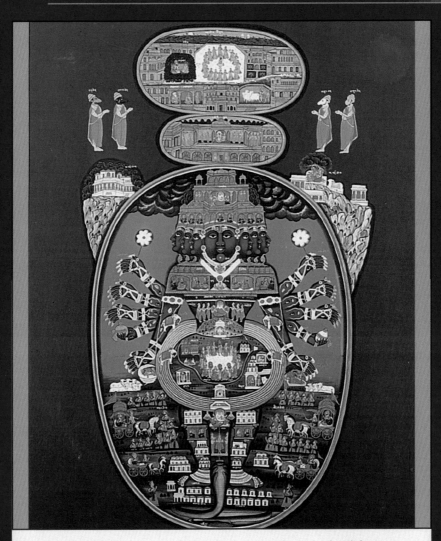

During the famous conversation between Arjuna and Krishna on the eve of battle in the Bhagavad Gita, Arjuna is permitted to view the god's cosmic form, which is not normally revealed even to the divine devas. Arjuna was able to glimpse this rare sight because his mind was, at that moment, so intensely devoted to God that he was able to see it through his eye of wisdom, or *divya chakshu*. According to the Gita, everyone is capable of achieving this level of concentration and devotion, which will allow them, too, to see Krishna's cosmic form. This nineteenth- or twentieth-century painting from the Rajasthan School, held in the Victoria and Albert Museum in London, depicts the cosmic form of Krishna.

Sita is known mainly as the wife of Rama, the hero of the epic Ramayana. She is revered as a model Hindu wife, who, despite facing terrible injustice, always remains loyal to her husband. In the story, when Rama is forced by his father into exile in the forest for fourteen years, he initially intends to leave Sita behind, so that she will not have to bear the discomfort of the exile. She threatens to commit suicide if Rama does not allow her to remain at his side. Later, after Rama has ascended the throne, Sita is kidnapped by the demon Ravana. Upon her release, the people accuse her of having had a romance with the villain, and to please his subjects, Rama considers banishing his wife. To prove her innocence, she throws herself upon a burning funeral pyre and emerges unharmed. This folio from a seventeenth-century version of the Ramayana depicts the scene in which Rama asks his brother Lakshmana to take Sita into the forest and abandon her, as punishment for her supposed relationship with Ravana.

early childhood (including birth, name giving, first taking out to see the sun, first feeding of rice, and the first haircut), these are not part of the individual's conscious journey toward spiritual liberation. Consequently, the first stage of life is not infancy but rather being a student of religion. It is called "the student stage" of life.

BIRTH AND PRE-BIRTH RITUALS

In the Hindu religion, there are several special rituals associated with birth. Among them are:

- *Garbhadana* (conception): This is a prayer said, asking the gods to help a child fulfill the parental obligation to continue the human race.

- *Punsavana* (protection of the fetus): This ritual is done during the third or fourth month of pregnancy, before the fetus is believed to be conscious. It is intended to bring out the unborn child's divine qualities.

- *Simantonnayana* (satisfying the craving of the pregnant mother): Done during the seventh month of the mother-to-be's pregnancy, this ritual is somewhat similar to a baby shower. Attendants say prayers for the healthy physical and mental growth of the coming child.

- *Jatakarma* (childbirth): This ritual formally welcomes the child into the Hindu family. Mantras are chanted to help bring the child a long, healthy life.

- *Nishkarmana* (taking the child outdoors for the first time): This rite of passage occurs four months after a Hindu child is born.

- *Annaprasana* (giving the child its first solid food): This ritual takes place during the seventh or eight month after a child's birth. There are detailed scriptural instructions that govern what foods should be given to the child and how.

In ancient India, upper-caste males were sent to the home of a *guru* (teacher) to study the Vedas and other religious works, along with the duties of their caste. The student stage began with a ceremonial investiture with the sacred cord, signifying the young man's second or spiritual birth. Students were expected to observe strict chastity. Refraining from sexual activity was so important that the Sanskrit word for celibacy, *brahmacharya*, is derived from the word for "student." On average, the student stage of life extended from between ages eight and twelve to about age twenty (though still being a student at age twenty-five was not uncommon). Females and lower-caste males were not given this type of religious education. Females in the learning stage of life remained at home and were trained in domestic work.

Although the ancient form of religious education still exists, few modern Hindus are educated in this way. The modern Indian school system is much like that of Great Britain or the United States. The emphasis is on modern, secular subjects, and education concerning religion is generally done at home. Both boys and girls are expected to attend school but, in many communities, boys and girls are taught in separate classrooms. Both young men and young women are eligible to go to Indian universities. The role of religion in public education is highly controversial—more on this in the final chapter.

In the *upanayana* ceremony, a Brahmin priest bestows a sacred cord on the student. The boy wears the cord over the left shoulder and around the right side of the waist under his clothing. This cord represents the initiate's second, or spiritual, birth, and signifies that he is now a man. Because their male children go through this ceremony, the three upper varnas are designated as the "twice-born."

The priest also bestows upon the initiate a *mantra* that is to serve as a focus for his spiritual life. The most commonly given mantra is the *Gayatri* mantra, taken from the Rig Veda. The name of this mantra comes from the Sanskrit poetic meter in which it is written. It calls upon the various realms of the cosmos (earth, air, and heavens) to join the reciter in acknowledging the beauty and gifts of the sun god, Savitar. Translated into English, it says: "OM, earth, atmosphere, heaven! Let us contemplate the lovely splendor of the god Savitar, may he stimulate our minds." The Gayatri mantra is to be recited daily, upon first seeing daylight, by male members of the twice-born castes. The upanayana ceremony concludes with a great feast to which family, friends, and members of the community are invited.

Female children do not have an upanayana ceremony. Marriage is the initiation into adulthood for daughters, although it is not unusual for the women of a community to get together to celebrate a girl's first menstruation (men are not invited to this ceremony).

The second stage of life is the householder state. The householder's life is oriented toward society, duty, marriage, and progeny (having children and perpetuating the family line). Traditionally, adult males work at their jobs and professions, while women take care of the home and children. Recent decades have seen the emergence of greater opportunities for women, but most Hindus still see the dharma of women as being centered more in the home than in a career.

Marriage is the beginning of the household life. Traditionally, almost all marriages were arranged by the families of the bride and groom. Contemporary life has changed that somewhat, but arranged marriages are still quite common. When asked about the role of love in marriage, a Hindu man once

NAMING A HINDU CHILD

The naming of a newly born Hindu child is a very important rite of passage, one that is described very specifically in Hindu scripture. The name chosen will have a special meaning, which, it is hoped, will help the child follow the path of spiritual righteousness.

Hindus frequently name their children after gods, saints, wise men, holy persons, and the various names of the incarnation of God. They believe that the use of such names will serve to remind both the person named and others who meet him or her of God.

replied: "We do not marry the woman we love; we love the woman we marry."[11]

Before the families commit to any final arrangements for the marriage, an astrologer is consulted. He will search the horoscopes of the prospective bride and groom to see if there are any potential difficulties. He will often consult with the man and woman in a form of "pre-marital counseling." There are times when the astrologer will counsel against a marriage. It is not unheard of, even in modern times, for an engaged couple experiencing difficulties to ask an astrologer to locate the source of their incompatibility. Should the astrological analysis show that their marriage will result in an unhappy situation, they may well terminate their engagement.

If all goes well, the astrologer sets an auspicious date for the wedding. The wedding usually takes place in the bride's home before a sacred fire. The officiant is a Brahmin priest, of course. The bride and groom take seven steps around the fire, each step representing a commitment to one another. Finally, the groom places the bright red mark, known as the *tilak*, upon his new wife's forehead, indicating that she is now a married woman.

The third stage of life is that of "the hermit" (literally, "forest-dweller"), but in modern times, we might call this stage that of

THE DOT ON THE FOREHEAD OF HINDU WOMEN

The colored dot often seen on the foreheads of Hindu women has various names, including "*tilaka*," "*bottu*," "*bindiya*," "*kumkum*," and "*bindi*." The dot is a sign of piety, and it indicates to other people that the person who wears it is a Hindu. The dot is a symbol of the third eye—the one that is believed to be turned inward, toward God. Although both men and women do wear the dot, over time, it has been going out of fashion for men, and is now mainly confined to women. In past times, one could differentiate married women from single women by the color of the dots they wore: Unmarried women wore black marks and married women wore red. Today, however, women often wear dots that match the color of their saris, regardless of their marital status.

"the retiree." This stage of life is oriented to reflection and contemplation. The transition to this stage usually occurs relatively late in life. According to the ancient texts called the *Dharma-shastras*, it is appropriate only after the birth of one's first grandson, that is to say, after one has made sure that the male lineage will continue. In this stage, the retiree is relieved of all social responsibility and will be cared for by his or her family. Of course, the retiree has the corresponding obligation to live simply so as not to be an undue burden upon the family. Usually, a husband and wife will agree to take this step together. The stage of the retiree is not required, and some people never formally enter it, though they may informally ease into it as they grow older. Women often become retirees upon the death of their husbands.

The last stage, that of the *sannyasin*, or "renunciate," is the most radical. It entails making a complete break from society in order to pursue the spiritual path. It is a status beyond family or caste. The renunciate—who is almost always male—will leave his former life completely behind him, leave his family and relatives, his familiar surrounding, his home, and put himself entirely in the care of the divine. Sannyasins are expected to beg for their food and their simple clothing, but since it is regarded as very meritorious to give to a sannyasin, they are usually able to survive albeit in humble fashion. Some sannyasins are supported by a community, usually a different one from that in which they formerly lived. Since sannyasins are regarded as holy men, they often have followers whom they instruct and who will, in turn, provide for their needs.

According to the Dharma-shastras, a man can become a sannyasin after the birth of his first grandson. However, the great philosopher Shankara said that there were a few young men whose spiritual development was so great that they should be permitted to go straight from being a student to being a sannyasin.

The family may not always welcome a person's decision to become a sannyasin, since it is essentially a voluntary "death while alive" to the rest of one's relatives. There are those who do not want to lose their loved ones to the renunciate's life, and it is not unheard of for a man simply to leave his home and become a renunciate without telling his family. Though the life of the renunciate is one of the four acknowledged stages, only a small minority of people will ever enter it. It remains, however, a living option, and, therefore, one that every Hindu must consider, even if only to reject it.

Beyond the stages of life, Hindus also have precise rituals governing the treatment of the dead. Hindus cremate their dead, rather than burying them. It is considered auspicious to die in the holy city of Banaras, and to have one's ashes scattered in the sacred Ganges River. Many people move to Banaras with the express intent of dying there, and many families are willing to travel long distances to scatter a loved one's ashes on the Ganges.

THE CASTE SYSTEM

For several thousand years, the caste system provided the organizational structure of Indian society. Even Muslims and

RITES OF THE DEAD

Hindus generally cremate their dead. The body of the departed is given a bath and dressed in fresh clothes. Fragrant sandlewood paste is applied to the corpse, which is then decorated with flowers and garlands, followed by a small amount of gold dust sprinkled on different parts of the head and face. After some purificatory scriptural chants and worship rituals, the body is placed on the funeral pyre facing either north or south.

A close relative of the departed lights some kindling and walks around the pyre chanting a prayer for the well being of the departed soul. Then he lights the funeral pyre after touching the mouth of the departed with kindling.

In larger cities bodies are cremated in modern crematoria. The ashes are later put in a holy river or sea.

The body of a Hindu saint is not usually cremated but put in a grave or buried in water.

Quoted from: *http://www.hindunet.org/last_rites/index.htm.*

Christians were assigned a caste, since there was no way to function in Hindu society without one. Though there is much controversy in modern Hinduism about caste and its role in today's world, there is no denying that caste dominated the social life of India in ages past. Although legally abolished, it continues to be very influential, especially in the rural areas.

At the center of the caste system is the ideal of *Dharma*— "that which structures" nature and society, that is, the natural and moral order. Dharma is one of the richest words in the Sanskrit language. It is the Cosmic Order, the laws of nature and, by extension, the specific characteristics of things. It is the righteous and stable social order and, by extension, the specific roles and functions that constitute a society. Dharma for the individual is one's proper duty within the social order and thus within the cosmic order.

The duties and responsibilities of the caste system are described in the Dharma-shastras, which we might translate as "textbooks on law and duty." These books describe in detail how the proper Hindu community should be structured, what duties are expected of each person, and how each individual life should be lived. Even though Indian society has changed greatly in the two millennia since the time when the Dharma-shastras were written, modern Hindus still look for ways to adapt these laws to the contemporary world. They try to live in the spirit of the principles of the Dharma-shastras, even when their regulations can no longer be applied literally.

Dharma means "justice," but it does not mean "equality." That may seem strange to Westerners, who are used to equating the concepts of justice and equality. Here, justice means everything in its proper place, but not all places are equal. In actuality, this view of justice was once common in the West as well. It is what justice meant to the ancient Greek philosopher Plato, for example.

Jati, usually translated as "caste," is the vehicle by which one fulfills Dharma. Caste is defined by sociologists as "an endogamous occupational category determined by birth," which means one is born into a specific caste, one marries in that caste, one

(Continued on page 92)

THE LAWS OF MANU: AN EXCERPT FROM THE DHARMA-SHASTRAS

1. The great sages approached Manu, who was seated with a collected mind, and, having duly worshiped him, spoke as follows:

2. "Deign, divine one, to declare to us precisely and in due order the sacred laws of each of the (four chief) castes (varna) and of the intermediate ones.

3. "For thou, O Lord, alone knowest the purport, (i.e.) the rites, and the knowledge of the soul, (taught) in this whole ordinance of the Self-existent . . . , which is unknowable and unfathomable."

4. He, whose power is measureless, being thus asked by the high-minded great sages, duly honoured them, and answered, "Listen!"

5. This (universe) existed in the shape of Darkness, unperceived, destitute of distinctive marks, unattainable by reasoning, unknowable, wholly immersed, as it were, in deep sleep.

6. Then the divine Self-existent . . . indiscernible, (but) making (all) this, the great elements and the rest, discernible, appeared with irresistible (creative) power, dispelling the darkness.

7. He who can be perceived by the internal organ (alone), who is subtle, indiscernible, and eternal, who contains all created beings and is inconceivable, shone forth of his own (will).

8. He, desiring to produce beings of many kinds from his own body, first with a thought created the waters, and placed his seed in them.

9. That (seed) became a golden egg, in brilliancy equal to the sun; in that (egg) he himself was born as Brahman, the progenitor of the whole world.

10. The waters are called narah, (for) the waters are, indeed, the offspring of Nara; as they were his first residence (ayana), he thence is named Narayana.

11. From that (first) cause, which is indiscernible, eternal, and both real and unreal, was produced that male (Purusha), who is famed in this world (under the appellation of) Brahman.

12. The divine one resided in that egg during a whole year, then he himself by his thought (alone) divided it into two halves;

13. And out of those two halves he formed heaven and earth, between them the middle sphere, the eight points of the horizon, and the eternal abode of the waters. . . .

114. The laws concerning women, (the law) of hermits, (the manner of gaining) final emancipation and (of) renouncing the world, the whole duty of a king and the manner of deciding lawsuits,

115. The rules for the examination of witnesses, the laws concerning husband and wife, the law of (inheritance and) division, (the law concerning) gambling and the removal of (men nocuous like) thorns, . . .

117. The threefold course of transmigrations, the result of (good or bad) actions, (the manner of attaining) supreme bliss and the examination of the good and bad qualities of actions,

118. The primeval laws of countries, of castes (gati), of families, and the rules concerning heretics and companies (of traders and the like)—(all that) Manu has declared in these Institutes.

119. As Manu, in reply to my questions, formerly promulgated these Institutes, even so learn ye also the (whole work) from me.

(Continued from page 89)

performs the duties associated with that caste, and one dies in the same caste into which one was born.

Each jati has its own characteristic occupations, and its own religious and social practices. In traditional villages, each caste is governed by its own caste council. There are different duties for each jati. The Bhagavad Gita says: "Better do your own work imperfectly than do another's well."[12] It was considered a horrendous sin to do another's task, because that implied taking someone else's job away from him. In the caste system, everyone was assured a place in society; no one had to compete for a job. The flip side of the coin, of course, was that one couldn't compete to move up in caste system. Even today, the relations among castes are governed by deeply ingrained custom, not by supply and demand.

There are a great many different castes in India, but they are usually grouped into the four *varnas*: Brahmins, Kshatriyas, Vaishyas, and Shudras. Brahmins were priests and teachers, Kshatriyas were warriors and rulers, Vaishyas were producers and business people, and Shudras were servants or, today, the "working class."

There is a group below the four varnas. They were once called "Untouchables," and were forced to do the tasks no one else wanted to do. Mohandas Gandhi called them *Harijans* (meaning, "children of God"). The Indian government calls them "the scheduled castes," because a list (schedule) has been made of all the groups that belong to this category so that they might be given special attention and helped to progress faster.

Though the caste system does not fit well with American ideas about how a society should run, it has been a durable and successful way of organizing social resources in India. Its basic principles have found social support, not just from the upper classes, but equally from the lower classes. To the great surprise of Western political scientists and social analysts, caste did not fade away after India became a modern democratic nation. Instead, the castes transformed themselves into political action groups. This political use of caste identity has proved quite beneficial to the lower classes.

The basic metaphor underlying the caste system is one that likens society to the human body. As in the body, so too in society, each part must fulfill its own proper function if the whole is to prosper. The prosperity of the whole entails the prosperity of the

IN FAVOR OF THE CASTE SYSTEM

—Swami Vivekananda

The older I grow, the better I seem to think of caste and such other time-honored institutions of India. There was a time when I used to think that many of them were useless and worthless, but the older I grow, the more I seem to feel a difference in cursing any one of them, for each one of them is the embodiment of the experience of centuries. . . .

A child of but yesterday, destined to die the day after tomorrow, comes to me and asks me to change all my plans and if I hear the advice of that baby and change all my surroundings according to his ideas I myself should be a fool, and no one else. Much of the advice that is coming to us from different countries is similar to this. Tell these wiseacres, "I will hear you when you have made a stable society yourselves. You cannot hold on to one idea for two days, you quarrel and fail; you are born like moths in the spring and die like them in five minutes. You come up like bubbles and burst like bubbles too. First form a stable society like ours. First make laws and institutions that remains undiminished in their power through scores of centuries. Then will be the time to talk on the subject with you, but till then, my friend, you are only a giddy child."

Caste is a very good thing. Caste is the plan we want to follow. What caste really is, not one in a million understands. There is no country in the world without caste. Caste is based throughout on that principle. The plan in India is to make everybody Brahmana, the Brahmana being the ideal of humanity. If you read the history of India you will find that attempts have always been made to raise the lower classes. Many are the classes that have been raised. Many more will follow till the whole will become Brahmana. That is the plan.

Source: Available online at *http://www.sivanandadlshq.org/messages/caste.htm*.

parts. If a part does not perform its function, then the whole is weakened, and this is to the ultimate detriment of the parts. The metaphor of the "social body" was common in pre-modern Western social thought as well.

In this vision of society, everyone is important, but people are not all equal. There are different parts with different functions. Some parts are considered superior to others. However, even the lowliest part has great value in its proper place, because it is necessary for the functioning of the body. Everyone should remain in his or her place, but there is a place for everyone.

Just as our body has eyes, ears, arms, and legs, all different,

AGAINST THE CASTE SYSTEM

Caste System has been the bane of Hindu society for centuries. In terms of damage to human progress and suffering, it did much greater damage for a much longer period to a great many people than the slave system of the western world. The caste system was a clever invention of the later Vedic people, who found it to be a convenient way of perpetuating their religious distinction and social privileges.

The idea of keeping oneself away from unclean people is understandable in a society that was obsessed with the concept of physical and mental purity. Even in modern societies people would not like to interact with people who are physically unclean and are into wrong ways of living. But what was wrong with Vedic society was to attribute these qualities to a group of people irrespective of their individual distinctions and then deny them perpetually the right to lead a decent life through self effort. . . .

The caste system was responsible for the weakness of Hindu society and for the invasion and subjugation of Hindus by several foreign forces. The physically strong shudras were condemned to pure agricultural labor and menial jobs. They would have been more useful as fighters and soldiers and defended the land well against foreign invasions.

Source: Available online at *http://hinduwebsite.com/hinduism/h_caste.htm.*

yet each with its own necessary function, so society has many different types of people. We do not think of our bodily parts as equal: the eyes, the brain, or heart are much more prestigious organs than, for example, liver or spleen and certainly more than the feet. But "lower" parts are just as necessary as "higher" ones, and a malfunction in liver or spleen can lead to dire consequences. The goal is for the higher and the lower to harmoniously co-exist and mutually benefit each other. Relations among castes are governed by a network of mutual obligations and benefits, so that each caste contributes to the welfare of every other caste in a very real sense, even though each caste is socially distinct.

To those content to live within the caste system, the security of having a place is more important than social mobility. Although there is some social mobility within the caste system, it is limited. One may not move into a different caste, but one can improve one's lot in life, and earn additional wealth, by working hard at one's job. American society values mobility over security, perhaps because most people assume that mobility means upward mobility. If the United States were to experience a sustained economic downturn, we may come to value security more, even in our culture.

Caste is determined by karma. The specific caste of an individual is determined by his or her deeds in previous lives. Furthermore, how one acts in this life determines the characteristics of one's next incarnation. A belief in karma is critical to a belief in the fairness of the caste system, though one may certainly believe in karma and reincarnation without being committed to traditional Indian social structure.

In modern India, caste is less rigid and less powerful than it was in times past, though it is still a force to be reckoned with. Personal ads in Indian newspapers often mention caste as a prerequisite for a relationship. Many Hindus argue that the basic elements of the caste system, if not its exact structure, are a necessary part of any well-functioning social system.

7

Hindu
Popular Culture

Out of compassion for them,
I situated within the heart, certainly
destroy the darkness born of ignorance
with the radiant light of knowledge.

—Bhagavad Gita

Hinduism expresses itself through a vast variety of art forms, far too many to be reviewed in a single chapter. Therefore I have been selective.

Perhaps the most internationally well known of India's art forms is its sculpture. Around the world, museums and even private homes proudly display sculpted Hindu deities. For this reason, we will begin with sculpture. Next, we will briefly consider the ancient form of theater, followed by two art forms derived from it—namely, music and dance.

This chapter will conclude with three topics that fall within the realm of popular culture: the sacred cow, OM, and astrology. I refer the reader as well to the discussion of Hindu literature in Chapter 3, and to the discussion of temple architecture in Chapter 5. These last topics will not be included in this chapter.

SCULPTURE

Hindu sculpture is prominently displayed within temples, or on their exterior walls. The sculptures within a temple are typically used in worship, while those adorning the exterior walls function as decoration. Whether used as an object of devotion or as decoration, any sculpture may convey religious symbolism.

Hindu sculpture displays gods and goddesses, heroes and heroines, animals and foliage. Deities may have animal heads, or multiple arms or faces. While not realist, Hindu sculpture is not schematic or abstract. The female body, complete with jewelry, is voluptuously portrayed. Male figures, equally well proportioned, are generally lithe and supple rather than tense and muscular. There are also ferocious figures, which often remind one more than anything else of a Halloween mask.

In Hinduism, sculpted figures dance. Even though carved out of stone or metal, they convey movement and vitality.

The major gods and goddesses are the main figures portrayed within a temple. Here, one may find Parvati, exquisitely shaped and ornamented. She cuts a regal figure with a tall crown on her head. Her hands and arms gesture in various *mudras* (symbolic positions), soft and feminine but with clear authority. Or, perhaps the eyes alight on Vishnu, also wearing a tall crown. In each of his four arms he carries a symbol of his power. In most temples and shrines you will find a sculpted image of Ganesha, the elephant-headed god. He is heavyset, a rarity among Hindu deities, who tend to be portrayed as male and female ideals. His corpulence is the result of the sweet treats he loves to eat, offered to him by his many devotees. Durga is often shown vanquishing the buffalo demon, Mahishasura. Shiva dances wildly and energetically, yet with the serene face of a yogin. These are just a few of the sculpted images one might find within a Hindu temple.

There are deities on the exterior walls of a temple as well, but these are often minor deities. They are joined by vast numbers of human beings. Sculptures on exterior walls may be arranged in ascending rows, all the way up the sides of the tower. They are small, because there are so many of them, but they are all lovingly and gracefully carved. They often portray aspects of life which we would call secular, for example, war, social life, and romantic encounters.

The overriding impression left by Hindu sculpture is its sensuality. The human body may well be Hinduism's premier aesthetic form. Not only in sculpture, but also in theater and dance, the body is used to evoke moods ranging from melancholy to exuberance to prayerful adoration.

THEATER

In ancient India, theater, music, and dance were part of a single endeavor; they were not treated as separate disciplines. Actors danced for the duration of a play, accompanied by musicians. Although this ancient art form no longer exists, one could perhaps get some idea of what it was like by watching a contemporary *yakshagana* ("celebration of the celestials"), a rural form of stagecraft involving song, dance, and drama.

A yakshagana is performed by a team of fifteen to twenty actors who walk from village to village carrying their costumes and accessories on their heads. Such a troupe will travel twenty miles in an average day.

The performers are often housed in a temple. There they will erect an exceedingly simple stage using just four poles. While they don colorful costumes and put on their makeup, families arrive on foot or in bullock carts.

The play will likely be an episode from the Ramayana or the Mahabharata. The performance begins with puja to Ganesha, the remover of obstacles and bearer of good fortune. This is followed by antics performed by "clowns" known as *kodangis.*

Drums and cymbals accompany the performers, who will sing, dance, and act throughout the night. In addition to having strength and stamina, actors are expected to have a respectable knowledge of the Hindu scriptures.

All yakshaganas are free of charge. Temple funds or public funds are used to support the troupe.

In some temples, yakshagana is performed throughout the entire year except during the rainy season. In these cases, the troupe is generally named after the temple's deities.

DANCE

Dance is one of the disciplines that grew out of the ancient form of Indian theater. In the ancient theater tradition, the dancers mimed the story while the singers sang the dialogue. Instrumentalists accompanied both dancers and singers.

Dancers were traditionally attached to the temples. This association colored dance with a strong religious flavor. Indian religious dance attempts to evoke different moods in the audience.

Portuguese traveler Domingo Paes journeyed through the Vijayanagar kingdom from A.D. 1520 to 1522. He visited some intensive training sessions for young female dancers. His journal describes walls decorated with paintings depicting different dance poses, designed to help the aspirants to correct their steps. The king, Krishna Devaraya, took a keen interest in dance education and frequently visited these training sessions. According to Paes, the dancers were adorned with so many gold, pearl, and diamond ornaments that they required assistance in bearing their weight.

A dance consists of *mudras* (hand gestures), *abhinayana* (face and body expressions), and *gati* (footwork). Each area of India has its own unique dance traditions. A few of the most popular forms of dance are described below.

Bharata Natyam

This is one of the most important and one of the oldest of the classical styles of Hindu dance. It is a South Indian form of temple dance. Historically, it was used mainly in Hindu religious ceremonies.

Devadasis ("servants of God") are women who live in the temples. They are the traditional performers of Bharata Natyam.

Bharata Natyam is a solo dance. It is generally performed by one woman. A dancer will never turn her back to the gods whom she honors with her performance. The dance begins with *alarippu*, a gesture symbolizing that the body is an offering to the gods.

The movements of this dance style flow from a core pose in which the knees are turned outward and flexed, and the feet (also turned outward) are close together. The feet beat out complex rhythms while movements of the eyebrows, eyes, neck, shoulders, arms, and feet are executed in rhythmic succession.

Kathak

Kathak is the major dance style of northern India. It combines dance styles developed in the courts of the Mughal emperors with Hindu folk elements. It took on a distinctive form in the fifteenth and sixteenth centuries, when the story of Radha and Krishna became popular.

Kathak dancers hold their bodies straight. Intricate footwork consisting of walks, glides, and fast pirouettes give this dance form its vital, dazzling, and skillful appearance. Meanwhile, eyes, eyebrows, neck, and shoulders may etch out delicate movements. Kathak dances often express devotion to Krishna.

Kathakali

Kathakali is a dance-drama that is popular in the state of Kerala in southwestern India. The performance is a form of worship. The dancers act out stories from the Mahabharata and the Ramayana.

A vocalist sings or speaks the epic poetry, while the dancers express the meaning of each line with gestures that include finger pointing, sweeping body movements, and wide, circling arm movements. Drummers accompany the vocalist and dancers.

The heavily decorated costumes are oversized, to give the dancers a larger-than-life appearance. Dancers also wear heavy, mask-like face makeup, in colors that carry a symbolic meaning.

RADHA AND KRISHNA

The rapturous, blissful romance between Radha and Krishna is often interpreted as a symbol of the quest for union with the divine. Their love has been painted, sculpted, and narrated by innumerable poets. Here is the story of Radha and Krishna as told by Chandradhar Dwivedi, a Distinguished Professor of Pharmaceutical Science and a practicing Hindu Priest:

Krishna, the reincarnation of Vishnu, spent his childhood and early adulthood in Vrindavan. Krishna was a naughty and playful child. He would play tricks on his mother and steal butter. He was very fond of Radha, the daughter of a Gopa (cowherd). Radha and Krishna played, danced, fought, and grew up together. They wanted to be together and remembered for their love forever. But Krishna left Vrindavan to protect good will, virtues, and humanity. Radha waited for him. He overcame his enemies, and became king, and still she waited for him. He married and raised a family, and still she waited. Radha waited for Krishna for the rest of her life, but Krishna never returned. Although Krishna was never married to Radha, he said that her name would always be uttered before his, as a reward for her eternal love, and to symbolize the union of the human and the divinity.

Chandradhar Dwivedi, Ph.D.
Distinguished Professor and Head
Department of Pharmaceutical Science
College of Pharmacy
South Dakota State University
Brookings, SD 57007
A practicing Hindu priest

Dancers train for six to twenty years to learn the steps and movements of Kathakali dance. It requires extraordinary muscle control to contort the face to express certain emotions, and also to perform the leaps and spins.

Kathakali performances are often held outdoors. Today a performance may last for a few hours, but traditionally the dancers performed throughout the night, from around 7:00 P.M. to about 7:00 A.M.

Orissi

Orissi is a dance form from the state of Orissa in eastern India. Sculptures dating from the second century B.C. show dancers in poses characteristic of the Orissi dance style. Orissi developed from musical plays was commonly performed in temples and as village entertainment.

Once Jayadeva's *Gita Govinda* made its appearance in the twelfth century, it became the literary basis which supported the entire superstructure of Orissan dance. The *Gita Govinda* sings the praises of Radha and Krishna. Jayadeva himself sang these hymns in the temple of Jagannath at Puri, accompanied by a Devadasi named Padmavati. The devotees and pilgrims who visited the temple were captivated by their music, and it soon became the bedrock of Orissi dance.

Although it was once a group performance, Orissi today is a solo dance form, usually performed by a woman. It uses some of the same patterns and poses as Bharata Natyam, but in addition it includes curved body movements and jumps. The jumps add vitality to the Orissi style.

Manipuri

Manipur is a verdant, hilly region in extreme northeastern India. Dance and music is a way of life here, and Manipuri dance is very intricate and creative.

A dancer trained in the Manipuri style will bend his knees slightly and keep his feet facing forward. His body will form a figure eight shape, as he moves his chest and waist in opposite directions. The dancer's arms are employed in graceful, curved movements. Fingers trace delicate circles and curves in the air.

Many Manipuri dances have a story about Krishna as their theme. One particular type of Manipuri involves only male dancers, who perform jumps in time with the beat of drums, cymbals, and clapping.

MUSIC

Hindu music influenced the Beatles in the 1960s, and it has maintained a following in the West ever since that time.

The Origins of Indian Music

The origins of Indian music are inextricably intertwined with Hindu scriptures, mythology, and devotion. One of the four Vedas, the Sama Veda, deals with music. In Hindu mythology, Indra, the rain and storm god, rules over a heaven inhabited by *gandharvas* ("musicians"), *apsaras* ("female dancers"), and *kinnaras* ("instrumentalists"). Saraswati, goddess of learning and the arts, is usually portrayed holding the musical instrument known as the *veena*.

Music and religion were so intertwined in the Vedic Age that music was called *margi* ("destroyer of births"). The primary purposes of music were said to be to discipline the emotions and create a state of meditative consciousness.

The great sages, too, have played a role in the development of music. Narada is said to have brought the art of music to earth and taught it to humans. It is reported that another sage, Bharata, received a revelation from Brahma, god of creation, "for the joy of the universe." Bharata preserved the revealed knowledge in a detailed exposition on Hindu music and dance known as the Natya Shastra (treatise on dance, c. 200 B.C.).

Millennia ago, music and dance were combined in a single discipline called *sangeet*. Sangeet itself belonged to the field of stagecraft. Today, music, dance, and theater have differentiated into individual art forms.

The Components of Indian Music

Contemporary Indian music has two bases: *raga* and *tala*. Raga is the melody, and tala is the rhythm.

Whereas Western music divides an octave into twelve tones, Hindus subdivided the octave into twenty-two tones called *shrutis*. From these twenty-two shrutis were extracted melodies of five, six, or seven tones. These melodies were known as *ragas*, and Hindu music consists of improvisation on these ragas.

Each raga is meant to evoke a certain mood. In addition, each raga may be associated with a certain time of the day or a particular season of the year.

Tala (rhythm) is equally complex. The rhythm of a song revolves around repeating patterns of beats.

Classical Musical Traditions

There are two distinct musical systems in India today. Hindustani music is found in North India, whereas Carnatic music is characteristic of South India.

NARADA

The ancient sage Narada was loved and respected by all. He traveled about, preaching to people, uttering words of wisdom, and telling stories with an ethical message. In the Mahabharata, Narada tells King Yudhishthira to keep his army and weaponry ready, to be kind to his servants and prompt in paying their wages, not to overspend his earnings, and to provide the farmers with all the necessary facilities.

Narada appears in every Purana and all the major epics, always as a giver of sagely advice. In ancient India, no story was complete without him!

Yet Narada was not an advisor, an administrator, nor a teacher, in the conventional sense of any of those words. He was a musician, and he is said to have led many souls to salvation through his music. He sang songs of devotion and praise. Usually Narada makes his entry in a play or a story carrying a veena, a stringed musical instrument which he is said to have invented.

In Hindustani music, the classical Hindu musical tradition is blended with Arab and Persian music. Since the Muslims did not enter the southern sections of India, Carnatic music does not show Arab or Persian influences. Many Hindus believe that Carnatic music has its roots in the Sama Veda, without outside influence, but this is difficult to demonstrate because intermediate forms showing the historical development of South Indian music are lacking. Carnatic music typically consists of devotional songs sung for deities.

Musical Instruments

Of the many musical instruments native to India, the *sitar* and the *tabla* are best known in the West. The sitar is a stringed

RAGAS EXPRESS THE MOODS OF THE HOURS

"Ragas sung before dawn are slow, dignified and full of pathos. Thus the Rag Jogia meaning 'a mystic' very appropriately belongs to that period before sunrise when ascetics in India are given to religious meditation. The Rag Bhairau is devoted to the morning praise of Shiva. Then comes Asavari, sweetly devotional and pleading.

Again from noontime on to four o'clock the tunes suggest coolness and repose in the tropic heat of the afternoon. Sarang, sung at midday, is reminiscent of Megh Rag of the rainy season, and has a gliding style which is refreshing and soothing. The melody called Talang—sung at about three in the afternoon is dreamily smooth, light-hearted and lyrical in character.

There is again a touch of pathos in the tunes of the twilight hour suggestive of evening prayers or longing for the absent loved one. Then follow evening melodies, sparkling and romantic.

After midnight come melodies impressive, proud and sorrowful. There is Malkaus, slow in style and majestic in sorrow. It throbs with grief and its theme is usually a form of elegy or love-lament. Durbari kaura too is wrapped in melancholy dignity. Its haunting plaintive sweetness has a mystic quality."

From Ragini Devi, "Hindu Conception of Music," *www.geocities.com/Athens/Academy/5185/1-6.html*

instrument, somewhat similar in appearance to a guitar, but it has a round gourd for a body instead of the hourglass-shaped guitar body. It is the most popular instrument in North India. The sitar has five main strings plus two drones. It became popular in the West through the playing of internationally known sitar artist Ravi Shankar (b.1920).

The oldest Indian instrument is the drum. The tabla is a metal

RAVI SHANKAR

Ravi Shankar is a sitar player and a composer. He is known as the man who brought Indian music to the West. Former Beatle George Harrison calls him the "Godfather of World Music," a reference to the fact that his talents were not limited to Indian musical forms, but included jazz and other forms of Western music as well.

Shankar studied Hindustani classical music under the tutelage of Ustad Allauddin Khan. Khan was Shankar's guru, and Shankar was Khan's disciple. This was the traditional way of becoming a master musician in India.

As a young man, Shankar wrote scores for Indian ballets and movies. In 1952, he played for virtuoso American violinist Yehudi Menuhin in Delhi. Menuhin was impressed with both Shankar and Indian music. This was the beginning of Shankar's international fame. Just ten years later, Shankar opened the Kinnara Music School in Bombay.

Both Indian music and jazz highlight improvisation. Shankar explored the relationship between the two musical forms in his 1962 album *Improvisations*. In 1966 he played his first sitar-violin duet with Menuhin, and repeated the collaboration the following year as the showpiece performance for the Human Rights Day celebration at the United Nations.

His 1966 meeting with George Harrison brought him into contact with hippie culture, and he played at Woodstock in 1969. He objected to the drugs at Woodstock, however. While he and Harrison have maintained their friendship through the years, Shankar refused to appear at pop festivals after Woodstock.

Shankar continued to perform both within India and internationally in the following decades. He has received countless honors including eleven honorary doctorates and India's highest civilian award (1981).

drum which can be tuned by means of special kinds of coating given the skin. It is commonly seen as one half of a two-piece drum set. The other drum is known as the *dagga*. The dagga is made of wood, and it cannot be tuned.

Other instruments used in Indian music include several additional types of two-headed drums (the *dholak* and the *mridanga*), a small reed organ (the *harmonium*), a wind instrument similar to a clarinet (the *shehnai*), and several additional types of stringed instruments, one of which (the *sarangi*) is played with a bow. The veena is a zither with gourd resonators. Small hand cymbals known as *karatals* are used in devotional music. The *shankha* is a conch shell. It is blown when the door of a temple altar is opened.

POPULAR CULTURE
The Sacred Cow

In India, monkeys searching for food may be encountered in temples, and even taxis take care to avoid cows wandering in the streets. Whether in philosophy or in daily life, animal life is not strictly separated from human life. Animals are treated with a kindness thought sentimental in the West. Animals are even associated with divinity. Ganesha has an elephant head; Hanuman is a monkey. All the major gods and goddesses have animal mounts. Hinduism's reverence for animals is partially due to the belief in reincarnation, which holds that an animal may one day be reincarnated as a human being, or even as a god.

Cows receive special veneration. From ancient times, cattle symbolized fertility and wealth. In rural India, cows provide milk, butter, cheese, and *ghee* (clarified butter used in sacrifices). They provide fuel (dried dung) and the companionship associated with household pets in other cultures. They are decorated and proudly displayed on certain festival days. After one's own mother's milk, they are the next source of nourishment provided to a child. Hence they are *gau mata*, "mother cow," and harming them is considered equivalent to the harming of one's own mother.

The Sacred Syllable OM/AUM

The sacred syllable *OM* is another well-known Hindu symbol. So pervasive is it that many world religion textbooks use the OM (written in the Devanagari script used in both the ancient Sanskrit and modern Hindi languages) as the symbol of Hinduism, parallel to the way in which the cross is used as the symbol of Christianity.

The OM goes back to late Vedic times. Many ritual specialists came to believe that the power of the Vedic hymns resided not so much in their specific content but in the very sounds that they made. Many Hindus even today believe that sound and vibration are at the very core of what makes up the universe. The sounds of different syllables become the various powers that make up the world around us.

According to the ancient Sanskrit grammarians, the "O" or "AU" is the broadest and most rounded utterance the voice can make; the "M" is the most narrow and closed. In the process of pronouncing the syllable, the whole range of articulate sound is (at least in theory) encompassed. Since all sounds are to be found in OM, it follows that all words are included and, if all words are included, then all truth and wisdom, and in particular the words of the Vedas, are included as well. For that reason, OM is used at the beginning of sacrifices, meditation, prayers, and before performing yoga. Chanting OM as a mantra is believed to bring about mental and emotional calm, to overcome obstacles, and to enhance understanding.

Jyotish (Astrology)

Hindu astrology (*Jyotish*) is a branch of Vedic knowledge, and, thus, it is often called Vedic astrology. It is a sacred science in India. While it shares the twelve signs of the zodiac, the planets, and the astrological houses with Western astrology, it is unique in many other ways.

In Hindu astrology, the signs of the zodiac are strictly identical to the constellations, so that the sign Aries begins when the sun arrives at the constellation Aries. This is called the sidereal zodiac. The West uses what is known as the tropical zodiac, which defines Aries as the place of the spring equinox. Due to an astronomical phenomenon known as the "precession of the equinoxes," the date of the sun's entry into the constellation Aries and the date of the spring equinox have been slowly diverging, with the spring equinox now coming about a month after the sun's entry into the constellation. This means that the beginning of Aries in Hindu astrology now occurs on the boundary between Aquarius and Pisces in Western astrology. Likewise, someone with a sun sign in Virgo according to Western astrology will have a sun sign of Leo or perhaps Cancer in Hindu astrology.

Both the Western calendar and Western astrology are based on the movements of the sun. Western astrology is solar astrology. Jyotish, on the other hand, is a synthesis of lunar and solar astrology, with the moon often playing a more prominent role than the sun. A person is born when the moon is in a certain *nakshatra* or "lunar mansion," and this position is believed to be very influential with respect to a person's destiny. One's nakshatra is considered to be even more important than one's sun sign.

Hindu astrology was initially a lunar astrology. Solar astrology did not become significant until the time of Alexander the Great. Alexander's conquests opened the door to an exchange of ideas between Hindus and Greeks. As a result of this exchange, Hindu astrology adopted the twelve sun signs which the Greeks had inherited from the Babylonians. Greek influence also precipitated the first Indian star charts for individuals. Prior to the time of Alexander the Great, Hindu astrologers used their skills to predict the best times for rituals, or to make general predictions regarding the fate of large numbers of persons, the success or failure of wars, or the fortunes of kingdoms. After the time of Alexander, they began to pay attention to the everyday lives of ordinary people.

The Hindu astrologer divides the zodiac into many different types of parts. The most popular method is to divide the entire zodiac into 108 sections, each a little over three degrees in length. Each section then is given the attributes of the twelve signs in order so that one has a sequence of 9 x 12 signs. It is then possible to rearrange the planetary locations to fit the new sequence of signs. This is called a *navamsa* horoscope.

ASTROLOGY

Hindu, or Vedic, astrology differs somewhat from the type of astrology practiced in the West. Although the names of the zodiacal signs are the same in both India and the West, the gods and forces associated with the signs are quite different.

Vedic astrology is different from Western astrology mainly because it uses the fixed zodiac rather than the moving zodiac. Most people's "sun sign"—the one you can find in the newspaper every day—is usually one sign back when the chart is refigured using Vedic astrology. That means that, using the Vedic system, you are most likely no longer the sign you always thought you were. However, if you were born within about the last five days of a Western sign month, you will probably have the same sign under the Vedic system.

This chart illustrates the signs of the zodiac used in India.

VEDIC ZODIACAL SIGNS						
SIGN	SANSKRIT	NAME	TYPE	SEX	MOBILITY	LORD
Aries	Mesha	Ram	Fire	M	Movable	Mars
Taurus	Vrishaba	Bull	Earth	F	Fixed	Venus
Gemini	Mithuna	Couple	Air	M	Common	Mercury
Cancer	Karkata	Crab	Water	F	Movable	Moon
Leo	Simha	Lion	Fire	M	Fixed	Sun
Virgo	Kanya	Virgin	Earth	F	Common	Mercury
Libra	Tula	Balance	Air	M	Movable	Venus
Scorpio	Vrishchika	Scorpion	Water	F	Fixed	Mars
Sagittarius	Dhanus	Bow	Fire	M	Common	Jupiter
Capricorn	Makara	Alligator	Earth	F	Movable	Saturn
Aquarius	Kumbha	Pot	Air	M	Fixed	Saturn
Pisces	Meena	Fishes	Water	F	Common	Jupiter

Both Western and Hindu astrologers pay attention to the movements of the sun, moon, Mercury, Venus, Mars, Jupiter, and Saturn. These are the planets and luminaries visible to the naked eye. Western astrologers also use the more recently discovered planets of Uranus, Neptune, and Pluto. Hindu astrologers generally do not consider these latter planets in their calculations.

There are also two invisible astronomical points which lie 180 degrees from one another, at the points where the annual path of the sun and the monthly path of the moon cross over each other. This generally has no visible significance unless, as occasionally happens, the sun and moon either occupy the same point at the same time (in which case there is a solar eclipse), or they occupy the direct opposite points at the same time (in which case there is a lunar eclipse). In Western astrology, these are known as the lunar nodes, or the dragon's head and the dragon's tail. (Mythologically, the nodal points are the two halves of the dragon which swallows the sun during an eclipse.) A Western horoscope almost always has the nodes plotted on it, but they are not considered as important as the sun, moon, and planets. Hindu astrology, on the other hand, believes that these points, which they call Rahu and Ketu, are equal to the planets in their influence.

Even in modern India, astrology plays an important role in guiding daily life and in setting dates for important events. Most Hindu births will be plotted on a horoscope and in some parts of India, one's horoscope functions like a birth certificate. Many Hindus attribute the low divorce rate in Hindu marriages to the fact that an astrologer is consulted to match the charts of the prospective bride and groom. Most Americans would ridicule a public official who consulted an astrologer, but many Indians would thank him for being so careful in the performance of his duties. Even among the intellectual elite, knowledge of modern Western science has done little to undermine the social status of India's astrologers.

8

Hindu Holidays

Spiritual persons partaking of vegetarian remnants offered in sacrifice unto the Supreme Lord get relief from all varieties of sins; but those who prepare food for their own consumption, those sinners eat only sin.

—Bhagavad Gita

indu holidays often correspond to significant events in nature, events that are reflected in the Hindu calendar. Because of this, it is worth taking a brief look at the Hindu calendar and the country's seasonal profile.[13]

Like the calendars used by most traditional peoples, the Hindu calendar is based on the cycle of the moon. The lunar month begins with the new moon and continues through the day of the full moon to the appearance of the next new moon, which begins a new month. The duration of a lunar month is either twenty-nine or thirty days.

Each lunar month is divided in half: The time from the new moon to the full moon is called "the bright half" of the month, and from right after the full moon to the new moon is called "the dark half" of the month. It is generally considered luckier to begin important projects during the bright half of the month.

Since a month defined by the moon is a little shorter than the months of the solar calendar used in the West, twelve lunar months total about 354 days. Periodically, the Hindus insert an extra month, called *Adhik*, to keep the traditional lunar year in step with the solar year. Modern India uses the Western (Gregorian) calendar for official purposes and international relations, but continues to observe the traditional calendar as well.

A culture's holidays often correspond to seasonal changes or characteristics. However, as a tropical country, India does not have the clearly defined four seasons that countries in temperate climates have. Instead, Indians commonly observe six seasons of two months each. Since the phases of the moon are independent of the solar months, we cannot set up an exact correspondence between the Hindu months and the months with which we are more familiar. However, the following is an approximation.

THE HINDU CALENDAR
Phalgun (February–March)
Sarasvati's festival, the great Hindu holiday for students, takes place on the first day of the month of Phalgun.[14] Phalgun marks the beginning of spring. Sarasvati is the goddess of learning and

the arts. Images of Sarasvati are set up in schools and students make flower offerings. Textbooks are placed in front of the image with a prayer that the goddess will help the students master the books' contents.

Many women wear something yellow on Sarasvati's day. Yellow is associated with spring, and it is considered an auspicious color. Even the special foods for the day are tinged with yellow. One specialty is sweet yellow rice with almonds, cashews, and raisins. Another, called *karhi chawal,* is rice with a yellow curry.

The image of Sarasvati is not yellow. The goddess is completely white, white being the symbol of purity. She holds a stringed musical instrument (the *veena*) in two hands, the sacred scriptures in another hand.[15] She stands on a white lotus, the symbol of true knowledge. As the ruler of the intellectual and creative realms of being (rather than the material realms), Sarasvati avoids jewelry. She dresses in a simple white sari and rides on a white swan.

Temporary community shrines are erected in public places, and the image of the goddess is placed inside on a raised platform. Here, devotees congregate in the morning for *arati* and prayers. (*Arati* is a light offering, performed by waving a light in front of the image.)

In a temple, one might observe a priest putting chalk in the hand of a youngster and guiding the child's hand in writing the alphabet; this rite symbolizes initiation into the realm of knowledge. In fact, some parents will delay their child's entry into school until this special day arrives.

Another extremely popular holiday takes place on the day of the full moon of Phalgun. *Holi* originally celebrated the grain harvest, but today it is associated with hijinks, practical jokes, and good humor. It is said to commemorate Krishna as a young boy. The child Krishna was known as a continual prankster. People get into the spirit of the holiday by spraying colored powder and colored water on each other. Children with access to Western-style toys shoot passersby with squirt guns.

The name of this holiday comes from a story about a prince named Prahlad. Prahlad was a devout worshiper of Vishnu. His father strongly disapproved and tried to make his son abandon his devotion to the god, but no matter what the king did, Prahlad remained steadfast, with the aid of Vishnu. Finally, the king had a demon named Holika attempt to lure Prahlad into a fiery furnace. Once again, Vishnu protected his devotee and the fire consumed Holika instead.

Chaitra (March–April)

On the ninth day of the bright half of Chaitra, Hindus celebrate Rama Navami, the birthday of Rama, the hero of the Ramayana. Hindus fast for various lengths of time during the first eight days of the month, and the Ramayana is recited from beginning to end. On the ninth day, people make offerings in the local temples to an image of Rama as a baby in a cradle.

Hindus believe that Rama was a real person, an ancient king. Although he is estimated to have lived in the seventh or eighth century B.C., Rama continues to be India's most popular culture hero today. Hindus believe he was an avatara (incarnation) of the great god Vishnu.

The Ramayana, which was written down by 400 B.C., remains a living story, recited by thousands of storytellers across India. As such, it has countless minor variations.

At one level, Rama is portrayed as a hero who marries a beautiful maiden, is banished from his kingdom in Ayodhya by evil cunning, conquers the kingdom of a powerful demon, rescues his abducted wife, and returns home to reign as a wise, righteous, and victorious king.

More sophisticated audiences may hear of his struggles to adjudicate fairly between the needs of his family and those of his kingdom, or of the tensions in his relationship with his wife. The countless minor variations on the Ramayana meet the needs of its countless audiences.

Behind all the celebrations and all the storytelling stands the figure of Rama, God who takes birth as a man, and a man who in his perfect embodiment of humanity sheds the grace of God abroad in the world. It would take a poet, certainly, to even begin to do justice to this combination of the human and the divine. Fortunately, India had one.

Valmiki, the sage-poet who authored the earliest version of the Ramayana, signaled the divine-human nature of Rama in this way: Mandodari, the wife of the demon Ravana, killed by Rama, is grieving over her husband. She exclaims that he was killed by a god whom he had mistaken for a mere human being.

Ironically, Valmiki puts an entirely different claim in the mouth of Rama himself. After the entire drama has played out, the great god Brahma comes to fetch Rama home to heaven. "Thou art Lord Narayana (Vishnu)," he says, "and we seek thy

BALI'S HINDUS CREATE A LIFE OF BEAUTY

Bali is one of more than thirteen thousand islands in Indonesia. Its physical geography is stunningly beautiful. Towering volcanoes, some still active, contain large lakes. These lakes provide water for irrigating the rice fields that are neatly terraced into the hillsides.

The first Europeans to set foot on Bali were Dutch sailors who arrived in 1597. They fell in love with the island, and when Cornelius Houtman, the ship's captain, prepared to set sail, half of his crew refused to leave with him.

Nonetheless, it is not primarily the physical geography of this island that supports Bali's booming tourist industry. It is the religious lifestyle of the people.

Religion is everywhere in Bali. There is no separation of sacred and secular, and no way to separate culture from religion. Temples are on the mountains and in the valleys, on the seashore and in the rice fields. The rice field temples are small shrines dedicated to Dewi Sri, the Rice Goddess. They are made of virgin bamboo.

Every village has at least three temples, one for religious festivals, a second for funeral and cremation rites, and a third dedicated to the Gods of Heaven. Processions wind their way toward the temples. Inside the temples people are making offerings to the gods.

The many art forms for which this island is justifiably famous—the shadow puppet plays, the dance-dramas, the music and architecture— are all expressions of the unique form of Hinduism found in Bali, which is home to the largest body of Hindus outside of India. The Balinese sing and dance and perform to entertain the gods. If people entry back into Vaikuntha." Rama replies, "What are you saying? I do not know anything! Am I Narayana? I think I am only a man . . . I am a human being."

Can God himself lose his God-consciousness? Yes and no. Yes, because Rama does not think of himself as "God" any more than he thinks of himself as "the king" (even though he truly is the king). He is as much an exile from the heavenly court as he is an exile from the Kingdom of Ayodhya. No, because in the deeper and truer sense of the term, Rama never loses his God-consciousness. God-consciousness is not thinking that one is God. That is just a thought, and not a very holy

are also pleased by the entertainment, that is wonderful, but art is first and foremost a form of worship.

The life of the people is itself a religious art form. On this island, a person might spend an hour weaving an offering of palm leaves and flowers. He might light a stick of incense, or sprinkle holy water. She might whisper a mantra as her hands make gentle, sacred movements.

Bali lies just south of the equator, so our summer is the middle of the cool season there. The Bali Art Festival occurs during the cool season. It features competition among music and dance groups from every village on the island.

The cool breezes make this the best time of the year for kite flying. Like everything else on Bali, kite flying is a religious rite. Kites carry the praises of the people closer to the heavens. They also delight and entertain the gods. No kite goes on its maiden voyage without first being consecrated by a priest in an elaborate ceremony.

The kites, which are often forty-five to fifty feet in length, may require as many as twelve persons to launch them. Made of bamboo and cotton, they are shaped like fish, leaves, and dragons. The colors of the kites are always black, red, white, and yellow, because these colors represent the Hindu deities.

Each kite carries two hummers. When the kite is airborne, these hummers make a pleasant humming sound that can be enjoyed by the people below and the gods above. In some cases, the tuning of the hummers is critical to the flying ability of the kite.

one at that. God-consciousness is having God's consciousness instead of ego-consciousness, "putting on" the mind of God, sharing in God's perspective on life, and manifesting God's wisdom and truth in one's actions. This Rama does from beginning to end.

Not so Ravana, who *does* seem to think that he is God. The demon, who represents egoism, rules the kingdom of Lanka with an iron hand, terrorizing both humans and animals. He even attempts to place himself above the gods. He asked Brahma to assure him that he would not be killed by any superhuman being, and Brahma acquiesced. Thenceforth no god could rein in his reign of terror.

Because he believed that he was far superior to humans and animals, Ravana omitted them from his list of those from whom he wanted protection. Thus, it was that Vishnu could defeat him by becoming a human being, and thus it was that a monkey could act as Vishnu's main accomplice in this task.

Asadha (June–July)

Asadha, the month that marks the beginning of the rainy season, corresponds to the Western months of June and July. The festival of *Ratha-yatra*, "drawing the chariot," is observed on the sixteenth day of Asadha. The holiday originated in the coastal town of Puri, where it became the custom on this day to erect an immense image of Vishnu on an enormous wooden chariot, bedecked with flowers, ribbons, and various precious offerings. Young men harness themselves to the chariot and pull it along the streets of Puri. Since those who pull it as it moves through the city are considered to be especially blessed by Vishnu, people rush up to take their turns pulling the great wagon. Still others throw more flowers and offerings on the chariot as it passes. Although the main festival takes place in Puri, it has spread to many other cities as well, where smaller chariots and images are pulled through the streets.

The name given to Vishnu during this festival is *Jagganath*, which means "Lord of the World." In older times, there were people who were so fervent in their devotion to Vishnu that they would throw themselves down under the wheels of the divine chariot and be crushed to death. This occurrence gave rise to the English word *juggernaut,* which refers to something enormous that crushes everything in its path. Modern celebrations do not permit this sort of self-sacrifice.

Shravana (July–August)

The full moon of Shravana marks the observance of *Raksha-bandhan.* The word *raksha* means "to protect" and *bandhan* means "to tie on" (consider the English words *bind* and *band*). On this day, it is customary for members of the household and close friends to tie a small band (a *rakhi*), often decorated with flowers, around each other's wrists to serve both as a symbol of protection and "to protect the bond" of friendship and family harmony. The head of a household may tie on the bands for his family, but most often it is the female relatives who tie the bands on their male relatives—usually sisters tying the band on brothers.

A traditional rakhi consists of a few simple strands of colored cotton or silk, perhaps interwoven with gold thread. Recently the market has been flooded with "designer" rakhis, very often bearing elaborate or flashy decorations. But no matter how simple or ornate the rakhi, the important thing is the special kind of love it represents. For Raksha-bandhan speaks to one of the deepest and noblest emotions in the human heart: the enduring bond of love between a brother and a sister. Sisters are expected to support and pray for their brothers, and brothers are expected to always stand by and protect their sisters.

Raksha-bandhan goes beyond the merely personal relationship between two individuals, however. Not only in Hinduism, but in other religions as well, the bond between brothers and sisters is seen as the cornerstone of society. Persons who are not related by blood, but only by faith, can and often do call each other "brother" or "sister" in religious settings. In the traditional world, the ability of all members of a society to see themselves as brothers and sisters was the basis for a smoothly functioning society.

Bhadrapada (August–September)

On the eighth day of Bhadrapada, which is the beginning of early autumn, the festival of *Janmashtami* is celebrated. This midnight holiday marks the birth of Krishna. According to the story, the powerful demon Kansa knew that Krishna was going to be born on Earth and wanted to kill him. To foil Kansa's plans, Krishna's devotees disguised the infant and hid him with a family of cowherders. Krishna then grew up among the cowherding people and was later associated with them in his sacred stories.

Worshipers of Krishna gather at the temple at midnight to honor the infant deity. An image of Krishna is washed with the products of a cow—milk, butter, and yogurt—all mixed with honey. Once it has been poured over the image of the god, the mixture is considered to be specially blessed by Krishna and is distributed among those present. An image of the infant god is then put on a swing and pushed back and forth by various worshipers while they sing hymns that express their love of Krishna.

Mathura, the town where Krishna is said to have been born, is filled with pilgrims during Janmashtami. They come from every corner of India. When the hotels are full, they camp in a park, or even on the road. Carts selling sweets, religious books, and pictures of Krishna spring up everywhere.

Ashwin (September–October)
Navaratri (also called "Ramalila" or "Durga Puja")

The first nine nights of the month of Ashwin are devoted to the celebration of *Navaratri* (literally, "nine nights"), a popular festival dedicated to the Goddess. India has always recognized a divine female principle (*shakti*). Shakti has many names, and many faces, for India's goddesses bring life, prosperity, and knowledge, but also punishment and death to demons and evildoers.

Navaratri celebrates the defeat of a buffalo-demon (*Mahishasura*) by a fierce goddess named Durga. Durga's defeat of Mahishasura is a popular Hindu story. Here is one version of the tale:

Mahisha defeated the king of the gods and usurped the celestial throne. All the gods were driven out of heaven. Their faces blazed with anger, and flames literally shot forth from their burning faces. At a single point, the energy of all the fires coalesced to form Durga.

Durga is a warrior goddess. Sitting astride a fierce lion, a weapon in each of her ten arms, she is an awesome combination of beauty and power. It was the gods who gave Durga her weapons and her magnificent lion. The lion's roar shook the three worlds. Though confident of their control over heaven, even the demons were awestruck.

Lithe and slender, Durga's power was not in her muscular physique but in her indomitable will. Durga rode out to meet Mahisha, who changed forms several times in an effort to elude her, but she caught up to him and beheaded him. Her victory seemed effortless, even playful.

During Navaratri, temples dedicated to the Goddess usually have a constant stream of visitors. Beyond that, there is no single way to celebrate Navaratri. Hinduism is neither monolithic nor centralized.

In northern India, especially in Varanasi (Banaras), nine days of fasting are followed by Ramlila ("Rama Drama"), traditional plays based on the Ramayana. In eastern India, especially in Bengal, the festival is known as Durga Puja ("worship of Durga"). Temporary temples called "pandals," built to house the Goddess, are erected in neighborhoods. A sense of competition pervades their planning and construction. Many are lavishly decorated.

During Durga Puja, galaxies of twinkling lights make colorful pageants out of the dingiest lanes, which probably remain plunged in darkness the rest of the year. India is not a wealthy nation, but money is no constraint. People donate generously for this popular festival.

Special sculptors work long hours to create the images of Durga that are used in the pandals and in the processions. The images are made of straw, bamboo, and clay. Multitudes throng the streets, feasting on holiday foods and gazing on the shimmering vision of Durga, who towers above the crowd as power personified.

In Tamil Nadu, in southern India, decorated shelves are set up in one corner of each home. The shelves will hold however many dolls the family wishes to display during Navaratri. Some families keep old-fashioned wooden dolls in chests and take them out for this occasion. Because there are no rules qualifying or disqualifying dolls for the doll shelf, traditional dolls may stand side by side with Barbie dolls.

The best known and most colorful celebrations of Navaratri occur in western and northwestern India, throughout Gujarat and in some parts of Maharashtra and Rajasthan. Here the villagers spend the nine nights of Navaratri dancing the Garba and Rasa, traditional dances characterized by vigorous yet graceful movements executed to vibrant music.

So popular are these two dances that competitions are held and prizes given to those judged to be the best dancers. The dancers' costumes are traditional, colorful, and exquisitely embroidered. Dances usually begin late in the evening and continue until early morning.

In the Dandia ("stick") dance, dancers hold decorated bamboo sticks in their hands. Each dancer not only performs a solo dance with his own sticks, but also strikes his partner's sticks in a complex rhythm. The dance begins slowly, but ends at a frenzied pace.

Garba, traditionally a women's dance, is a graceful, circular dance around a perforated earthenware pot containing a lamp. The word *garba* means "womb." The lamp in the pot represents life within a womb.

The women swirl, bangles jingling and jewelry gleaming in the soft light. As they dance, they clap their hands in a syncopated rhythm. Chitra Divikaruni, a poet of Indian extraction now living in the United States, describes a garba dance in which she participated:

> . . . The women dance alone
> a string of red anemones

flung forward and back
by an unseen tide. The old ones sing
of the ten-armed goddess.
The drums pound faster . . .
. . . Our feet glide
. . . our arms are darts of light, Hair,
silver-braided,
lashes the air like lightning.
The swirling is a red wind
around our thighs. Dance-sweat
burns sweet on our lips.
We clap hot palms like thunder . . .
Damp faces gleam and flicker in torchlight.
The smell of harvest hay
is thick and narcotic
in our throat. We spin and spin
Back to the villages of our mothers' mothers . . .

Diwali

Diwali, probably the single most important Hindu holiday, occurs at the end of the month of Ashwin. Even those Hindus who are not particularly observant at other times of the year will usually celebrate Diwali. Diwali is also one of the most widely celebrated of Indian festivals. It is celebrated throughout India, and in many other countries including Singapore, Thailand, Malaysia, Kenya, and Trinidad.

Diwali, the "festival of lights," commemorates Lakshmi, goddess of wealth, as well as the return of Rama and Sita from exile. Rama's return to the throne symbolizes the victory of good over evil. People place lighted lamps in every window of their homes to light the way for Rama and Sita's return.

Decorative designs called rangolis are painted on floors and walls. Relatives and friends gather to offer prayers and distribute sweets. Children set off firecrackers, which contribute to the theme of the victory of good over evil by symbolically reducing the latter to ashes.

Diwali is also dedicated to Lakshmi, goddess of wealth and good fortune. Merchants and businesspeople renovate and decorate their establishments. Women may purchase something made of gold or silver. In the villages, cattle are adorned, because cattle symbolize wealth in rural areas.

Hindus believe that Lakshmi walks through the fields and along the roads during Diwali, showering her blessings of plenty and prosperity everywhere. The joyous sounds of bells and drums float out from the temples. Inside, Vedic hymns are chanted. The worshiper expects to see the impenetrable darkness pierced by a blaze of light descending from heaven as golden-footed Lakshmi alights on earth in all her celestial glory.

Magh (January–February)

The night of the new moon of every month is called "the night of Shiva." The new moon between Magh and Phalgun, approximately the thirteenth or fourteenth night of the dark half of Magh, is called *Maha-Shiva-ratri,* meaning "the Great Night of Shiva." Shiva, "the auspicious one," is the unifier of opposites. He is both destroyer and creator. He is the celibate yogi, but he is also the creative power of sexuality. As Ardhanarishvara, he is portrayed as half female, half male. Overcoming the dualisms of self and other, of renunciation and passion, of male and female, and even of thought itself, he leads worshippers back to the undivided unity that is Hinduism's Ultimate Reality.

In Hindu iconography, Shiva may be sitting silent and still in yogic trance, or dancing wildly in a ring of fire. He may be portrayed as a solitary ascetic, as a married god accompanied by his goddess wife (and sometimes by his children as well), or as Pashupati, the "lord of animals." His most common representation, found in temples throughout India, is the Shiva Linga, or the phallus of Shiva, which is the symbol of creation, the beginning of everything.[16]

Devotees observe a strict fast on Maha-Shiva-ratri (many do not even take a drop of water), and keep vigil all night long. Offerings of flowers, grain, water, milk, and sacred bael leaves are made to the linga. Worshippers chant mantras, sing hymns in praise of Lord Shiva, and recite his thousand and one names. Many pilgrims flock to the sites of Shiva temples. Most of the ceremonies take place at night.

What is the purpose of the fast and the vigil? In Hindu psychology, "rajas," the active and outgoing tendency of the mind, is dominant in the perceptual activities of the daylight hours. This is the conscious level of mind. "Tamas," the lethargic and inert tendency of the mind, is present in sleep. This is the unconscious level of mind. Neither the conscious nor unconscious mind is capable of God-consciousness, which occurs at the superconscious level. In order to see God, one must subdue both rajas and tamas. Rajas is controlled by the fast, and tamas is opposed by the vigil. The mind is then focused on God by means of the rituals, hymns, and chants.

The ceremonies take place primarily at night because Shiva is cloaked in darkness. To see Shiva one must stop looking at objects, because God is not an object. In Hinduism, God is the unified consciousness that exists before consciousness divides itself into subject and object. Light implies perception of objects for us, and we regard non-perception of objects as night. So God, not being an object of perception, must be encountered in darkness.

NAMES OF OTHER MONTHS

Kartik, corresponding to the Western months of October and November, marks the beginning of late autumn. It is followed by Margashirsha, which is roughly equivalent to November and December on the Gregorian calendar. Paus (December–January) is the Hindu month marking the start of winter.

Adhik, the extra month that appears every few years to help regulate the seasons and months of the Hindu calendar, comes after the month of Chaitra, between spring and summer.

Vaisakha (April–May) is the Hindu month that stands at the beginning of summer, and the summer month of Jaistha corresponds to the Gregorian calendar's May–June.

In sum, the Hindu months, in order, with their rough

Gregorian equivalents, are as follows:

Kartik (October–November)

Margashirsha (November–December)

Paus (December–January)

Magh (January–February)

Phalgun (February–March)

Chaitra (March–April)

ELEPHANT-HEADED GOD BRINGS SUCCESS AND WISDOM

Ganesha is no Adonis. He is short and stocky. He has a protruding, potbelly tummy. He has an elephant head with big floppy ears and a trunk curling down to a bowl of sweets, his favorite food. This huge figure rides through the cosmos on a tiny mouse.

He looks like he should be the butt of a thousand jokes, but instead he is the recipient of thousands upon thousands of prayers. Ganesha is one of the most popular Hindu deities.

He is the god of success, the remover of obstacles. As such, he is invoked at the beginning of any important undertaking. Ganesha is also the god of wisdom, education, knowledge, and prosperity. He is the god of writers, and removes "writer's block." He is himself a writer, having broken off his right tusk and used it as a pen to inscribe the renowned Indian epic poem, the Mahabharata.

Ganesha's large elephant head symbolizes the *atman* (the "True Self" or "immortal soul"), which is the source of his wisdom. His human body signifies *maya*, the temporal or earthly existence of human beings. This latter is not as important as the atman, but is nonetheless filled with good things, like the sweet treats Ganesha loves to eat.

The mouse is the ego, which is less important than either the atman or earthly existence. It is merely the vehicle in which the atman rides through life.

If Ganesha looks somewhat incongruous and upside-down to us, it is because we are so accustomed to putting things in reverse order, feeding our ego first, our physical well-being second, and our soul last.

A popular tale tells how Ganesha got his elephant head. Ganesha, it says, was guarding the door to his mother's home when his father, Shiva, returned home. Because Shiva had been away so long, father and son did not recognize each other.

Enraged that a stranger was keeping him from entering his own

Adhik (extra month added periodically to align solar and
lunar years)

Vaisakha (April–May)

Jaistha (May–June)

Asadha (June–July)

Shravana (July–August)

Bhadrapada (August–September)

Ashwin (September–October)

home, Shiva cut off Ganesha's head. When his grief-stricken wife told him what he had done, Shiva replaced Ganesha's head with that of an elephant. In the end, Ganesha is blessed with super-sized wisdom.

This bizarre myth speaks of everyday situations. What father has not, from time to time, had trouble recognizing his own rapidly growing and changing son? What father has not been tempted to (figuratively) behead his own son by insisting overly much upon his own authority in his own home? On the other hand, what father has not regretted his hasty words and actions? What father has not been willing to take extreme measures to right his wrongdoing?

The myth insists that wisdom can be gained even in the midst of such distorted family circumstances. Indeed, while no one would want to deny the importance of good homes, it is true that many wise and successful persons were raised in less than perfect homes, by less than perfect parents. Perhaps that is because imperfect circumstances provide better training in the removal of obstacles than do perfect circumstances.

Ganesha's annual festival begins on the fourth day of the bright half of the lunar month of Bhadrapada (August–September), and lasts for ten days. Before the festival begins, clay statues of Ganesha are purchased and installed in homes. In streets and commercial establishments, community worship is offered to a life-size or even larger image, which has been installed on an erected platform or under a large tent.

The Ganesha images are decorated with ornaments, flowers, and lights. Offerings of sweets, coconut pieces, fruit, and other items are blessed and distributed among the devotees after the worship service.

On the last day of the festival, the jovial god receives a ritual sending-off as he leaves for his celestial home. The images are carried through the streets in procession, accompanied by singing and dancing, to be immersed in a river or the sea.

9

Memories

*My sole object . . . was to express the very strong
views I hold against all acts of violence. . . . My mission
in life is to preach and assist in securing the utmost
freedom for my country but never by violence.*

—Mohandas Gandhi

T he history of Hinduism can be broadly divided into two periods. The first of these extends from the Vedic age until around A.D. 1200. The second begins with the coming of the Muslims in the early thirteenth century and extends to the present.

In the first period, Hindus developed their own civilization and enjoyed political sovereignty within their own land. We have already traced the broad outlines of this first period in the second and third chapters, where we discussed, respectively, the foundations of Hinduism and the development of Hindu scriptures.

In this chapter, we will discuss the second period, during much of which Hindus lived under either Muslim or European (primarily British) rule. Although Muslim rule began earlier in some parts of India, historians typically date the beginning of substantial Muslim power in India to the beginning of the thirteenth century. Muslim power remained substantial until the middle of the eighteenth century, although a shadow of the Mughal Dynasty persisted for another century. The British gained substantial power in India around 1750 and maintained it for about two centuries. India regained her independence from foreign rule in 1947.

We turn now to a consideration of memories from the periods of Muslim and British rule that remain alive among Hindus today.

MEMORIES OF THE MUSLIMS

In about A.D. 1200, Muslim armies from Iran and Central Asia began a sustained incursion first into Afghanistan and northwest India and then into the entire northern half of India. Muslim rulers set up kingdoms, and the city of Delhi became particularly important. The Muslim sultanate of Delhi would, at its height, control the northern two-thirds of the Indian subcontinent.

From the first, there was great tension between the religions of Hinduism and Islam. Although Islam granted "People of the Book" (Christians and Jews in addition to Muslims) general tolerance, the Muslims' attitude toward Hinduism was quite different. Islam began with a fight against polytheism, and its cardinal tenet is that there is no god but Allah. Its attitude toward those it considers idolaters has sometimes been harsh. Many Muslims saw Hinduism as a form of polytheism and idolatry that had no redeeming value and deserved little consideration. Hindus, on the other hand, remember the Muslims as brutal and intolerant.

Conflict between Islam and Hinduism continues to the present day, often with tragic results. A recent episode was the destruction of a great mosque in the city of Ayodhya that was said to be built over the birthplace of the great epic prince, Rama. At the heart of the conflict are two radically different visions of both religion and society.

Hindus are very *inclusive* in their religious vision; they believe that all religions have truth in them and that all religions, sincerely and faithfully practiced, will lead to the same goal. Thus there is no need to force conversion from one form of religion to another. The Hindu vision of society, however, is *exclusive*. Each caste and each ethnic group has its own specifically defined role and place in a social hierarchy.

The Islamic vision is precisely the reverse. Muslims are far more exclusive in their religious vision. Although other monotheistic religions are acknowledged to have some degree of truth, no other religion is believed to have the fullness of truth possessed by Islam. Polytheists or non-theists are considered disbelievers. Muslim society, however, is more open and democratic than is traditional Hindu society. All ethnic, racial, and occupational groups are (at least ideally) considered equal in the sight of Allah. Differences in occupation or wealth have no religious significance.

There are important differences in values as well. Whereas Hinduism strongly values nonviolence, Islam is not opposed in principle to the use of the sword, to the slaughter of cows, or to meat-eating. Hindus consider these practices barbaric. On the other hand, Muslims abhor the use of images in worship, and the Hindu practice of bowing down before human saints or even inanimate objects.

Despite these important differences, the interaction between Hindu and Muslim has not always been hostile or negative. As the Islamic rulers settled in India, they soon recognized that they would have to learn to get along with their Hindu subjects in one way or another. Over the following centuries, Hindu and

THE TAJ MAJAL

It was Shah Jahan who ordered the building of the Taj, in honor of his wife, Arjumand Banu, who later became known as Mumtaz Mahal, *the Distinguished of the Palace*. Mumtaz and Shah Jahan were married in 1612 and, over the next eighteen years, had fourteen children together. The Empress used to accompany her husband in his military campaigns, and it was in 1630, in Burhanpur, that she gave birth to her last child, for she died in childbirth. So great was the Emperor's love for his wife that he ordered the building of the most beautiful mausoleum on Earth for her.

Although it is not known for sure who planned the Taj, the name of an Indian architect of Persian descent, Ustad Ahmad Lahori, has been cited in many sources. As soon as construction began in 1630, masons, craftsmen, sculptors, and calligraphers were summoned from Persia, the Ottoman Empire, and Europe to work on the masterpiece. The site was chosen near the Capital, Agra on the southwest bank of the River Yamuna. The five main elements: the *Darwaza* or main gateway, the *Bageecha* or garden, the *Masjid* or mosque, the *Naqqar Khana* or rest house, and the *Rauza* or the Taj Mahal mausoleum comprise the architectural complex. The actual Tomb is situated inside the Taj.

The unique Mughal style combines elements of Persian, Central Asian, and Islamic architecture. Most impressive are the black and white chessboard marble floor, the four tall minarets (40 m high) at the corners of the structure, and the majestic dome in the middle. On closer look, the lettering of the Qur'an verses around the archways appears to be uniform, regardless of their height. The lettering spacing and density has been customized to give this impression to the beholder. Other illusionary effects have been accounted for in the geometry of the tomb and the tall minarets. The impressive *pietra dura* artwork includes geometric elements, plants, and flowers, mostly common in Islamic architecture. The level of sophistication in artwork becomes obvious when one realizes that a 3 cm decorative element contains more than 50 inlaid gemstones.*

* Quoted from: *http://ce.eng.usf.edu/pharos/wonders/Forgotten/tajmahal.html*.

Muslim neighbors came to recognize human virtues in one another, whatever their religious differences. Mutual mistrust evolved into tolerance and often, in individual cases, even became close friendship.

More recently, however, tensions have mounted between Hindu nationalists on the one hand, and Muslims who resent their "intolerant" image on the other. Muslims believe that the history of their rule of India has been unfairly slanted to give the impression that they were intolerant. Hindus, on the other hand, resent the critical examination of their own culture heroes. An

HINDU MEDICINE

Ayurveda, or "the science of life," is the name for Indian medicine. It is a holistic system that uses natural herbs and other plants to cure diseases. It covers many of the same fields as Western medicine, seen below with their Indian names.

- Agada Tantra (antidote method)
- Chikitsa (general medicine)
- Dehavritti (physiology)
- Dravyavidya (medicine and pharmacology)
- Kaumara Bhritya (pediatrics)
- Nidana (diagnosis)
- Pasu Vidya (veterinary science)
- Rasayana (tonics and rejuvenation)
- Salya (surgery)
- Stritantra (gynecology)
- Urdhvanga (diseases of the organs of the head)
- Vajikarana (sexual rejuvenation)

Hindu medical practitioners believe that health can be achieved through the balance of different bodily and spiritual energies (including, in particular, the *doshas,* or bodily humors). This balance

American scholar recently completed a book on Shivaji, a Hindu hero who defeated the Muslims and established an independent kingdom in the seventeenth century. The publication of his work by Oxford University Press provoked a riot on the part of Hindu demonstrators against what they viewed as the defamation of one of their heroes.[17]

Because emotions on both sides of the issue run high, it is hard to gauge the amount of negative or positive influence exerted on India by Islam. About the best we can do is to list specific positive contributions by both sides during the centuries of Muslim rule.

may be brought about in many ways, which are chosen based upon the lifestyle and character of the person being treated.

Hindu physicians have made many contributions to the progress of modern medicine, a few of which include:

- *Bhoja Prabandha*: This document describes a successful brain surgery performed by a Hindu in A.D. 927.

- *Chanakya*: The Hindu scholar Arthashastra described post-mortem examinations in this piece of writing.

- *Charaka*: In the 500 B.C. writing *Charka Samhita* (*Handbook of the Physician*), among the medical advances discussed are the anatomy of the human body, along with techniques for both diagnosis and treatment, as well as a list of animal, mineral, and plants needed to prepare various medicines.

- *Jaluka Prayog*: Agni Karma Vidhi described how to purify blood, and also demonstrated the use of heat and light as a treatment that eliminates the need for surgery.

- *Shushruta*: Around 600 B.C., Shushruta performed plastic surgery; his writings also mention some 120 kinds of surgical instruments and more than 300 methods for performing surgery on humans.

The Muslim rulers, particularly those of the Mughal Dynasty (1527–1858), sponsored beautiful art and architecture. The very symbol of India, the Taj Mahal in Agra, was completed in 1653 by a Muslim ruler, Shah Jahan, as a tomb for his favorite wife. Mughal paintings, influenced by Iranian models, are exquisite productions. Interestingly, their subject matter portrays as much Hindu mythology and society as it does Islamic themes and court life.

In the area of religious thought and practice, Hinduism developed still further adaptations. Paralleling Islamic theology, love given to a supreme personal God became more and more important. Devotional religion, emphasizing *bhakti*, the surrender of self in faith and devotion, became the centerpiece of Hindu religious life. People like Caitanya, a devotee of Krishna, and Tulsidas, who was devoted to Rama, imparted a new energy to Hinduism.

Even in the more intellectual planes of religion, Hinduism and Islam had fruitful interaction. Muslim mystics—the Sufis—and Hindu yogins found much common ground in spiritual practice. Sufism had already developed versions of the way of works and the way of knowledge, so the two religions enriched the practices of each other. Sufism would become and still remains an important expression of Muslim religiosity in India.

Some went even further and attempted to see commonalities or even a unity between Hinduism and Islam, different as these two religions might appear on the surface. The great Mughal emperor Akbar (who ruled from 1556 to 1605) promoted a "Divine Faith" that drew upon a purified version of all the religions known to him. Though it gained no lasting foundation, it nevertheless revealed a broad tolerance that was a high point of Hindu-Muslim relations. Akbar's successor, Aurengzeb, sought to undo all that Akbar had done and to enforce a strict version of Islam that excluded any cooperation with Hindu doctrine.

A more successful religious enterprise was the religion of Sikhism. Nanak (1469–1539), the great disciple of an Indian master named Kabir, was inspired to find the "true religion" behind both Hinduism and Islam. It would be wrong to think of

Nanak as trying simply to combine these religions, however. First, Sikhs believe that Nanak received a new and separate revelation from God. Second, Nanak held that both Hinduism and Islam were only partial reflections of one truth that lay behind them. He practiced Hinduism among Hindus and Islam among Muslims to demonstrate that there was no real contradiction between them, since they both proceeded from the one Divine Source. Nanak's Sikhism was extensively persecuted by the more fanatical Muslim rulers, for both religious and political reasons. However, Sikhism remains a very important religion in India and has spread to other parts of the world as well.

MEMORIES OF THE BRITISH

The British arrived in India in the late 1600s in the form of the East India Company, a trading corporation that was backed by the English government. Throughout the 1700s, British diplomacy and duplicity gave the British the ability to play one Indian prince against another. A prominent but controversial figure in this tangled intrigue was Britain's Warren Hastings, whose political and military efforts ensured that Great Britain would be the dominant European power in India, poised to replace the ever-weakening Mughal Empire centered in Delhi.

Eventually, the British Parliament essentially took over the East India Company, which would come to be associated with some of the great names of late-eighteenth- and nineteenth-century English history. Lord Charles Cornwallis would demonstrate that his loss at the siege of Yorktown in the American colonies (the defeat that ultimately won the Americans their independence from Great Britain) was something of a fluke in an otherwise very distinguished military career. Arthur Wellesley proved his military genius in India before he was sent to fight the French in Spain and then to take on French Emperor Napoleon Bonaparte as the Duke of Wellington. The philosopher John Stuart Mill was a civil servant in the East India Company, as was the noted English man of letters, Thomas Babington Macaulay (pronounced *Macullah*).

Macaulay, in fact, played an important role in English attitudes toward Indian culture. He wrote a short document that came to be called "The Macaulay Minute." A *minute* in this context meant a "memorandum" and was used in the same sense in which we speak of "the minutes of a meeting." His memo showed an utter disdain for everything traditionally Indian and urged the British officials in India to do all they could to Westernize their subjects. He said, "We must at present do our best to form a class of persons, Indian in blood and color but English in taste, in opinions, in morals, and in intellect." [18] Ironically, it would be precisely those Western ideas, such as liberty and equality, that

MACAULAY'S MINUTE ON INDIAN EDUCATION

February 2, 1835

As it seems to be the opinion of some of the gentlemen who compose the committee of Public Instruction, that the course which they have hitherto pursued was strictly prescribed by the British Parliament in 1813, and as, if that opinion be correct, a legislative act will be necessary to warrant a change, I have thought it right to refrain from taking any part in the preparation of the adverse statements which are now before us, and to reserve what I had to say on the subject till it should come before me as a member of the Council of India.

It does not appear to me that the Act of Parliament can, by any art of construction, be made to bear the meaning which has been assigned to it. It contains nothing about the particular languages or sciences which are to be studied. A sum is set apart "for the revival and promotion of literature and the encouragement of the learned natives of India, and for the introduction and promotion of a knowledge of the sciences among the inhabitants of the British territories." It is argued, or rather taken for granted, that by literature, the Parliament can have meant only Arabic and Sanscrit [sic] literature, that they never would have given the honorable appellation of "a learned native" to a native who was familiar with the poetry of Milton, the Metaphysics of Locke, and the Physics of Newton; but that they meant to designate by that name only such persons as might have studied in the sacred books of the Hindoos all the uses of cusa-grass, and all the mysteries of absorption into the Deity. This does not appear to be a very would inspire Mohandas Gandhi to start the movement that would one day undo British rule in India.

The resentment that Indians, both Hindu and Muslim, felt against the British finally exploded in 1857. In the West, the rebellion is commonly called "the Sepoy Mutiny" (a *sepoy* was an Indian soldier serving in the army of the East India Company), but in India, it is referred to as the "First Struggle for Independence." In this incident, a group of sepoys refused to use bullets that were supposedly greased with animal fat— offensive to Hindus if it were beef grease and offensive to both Hindus and Muslims if it were pork grease. When the

satisfactory interpretation. To take a parallel case; suppose that the Pacha of Egypt, a country once superior in knowledge to the nations of Europe but now sunk far below them, were to appropriate a sum for the purpose of "reviving and promoting literature, and encouraging learned natives of Egypt," would anybody infer that he meant the youth of his pachalic to give years to the study of hieroglyphics, to search into all the doctrines disguised under the fable of Osiris, and to ascertain with all possible accuracy the ritual with which cats and onions were anciently adored? Would he be justly charged with inconsistency, if, instead of employing his young subjects in deciphering obelisks, he were to order them to be instructed in the English and French languages, and in all the sciences to which those languages are the chief keys?

The words on which the supporters of the old system rely do not bear them out, and other words follow which seem to be quite decisive on the other side. This lac of rupees is set apart, not only for "reviving literature in India," the phrase on which their whole interpretation is founded, but also for "the introduction and promotion of a knowledge of the sciences among the inhabitants of the British territories,"— words which are alone sufficient to authorise all the changes for which I contend.*

* The full text of this document can be found in the Appendix.

British officers gave them direct orders, the sepoys revolted. The rebellion soon spread throughout North India. There were brutal massacres on both sides, but, in the end, the British prevailed because of their greater discipline and the inability of the various parts of the Indian population to rally to a common cause.

As a result of the conflict, in 1858, the East India Company, which had become something of a fiction anyway, was officially dissolved. In 1878, Queen Victoria was proclaimed "Empress of India." India became known as "the jewel in the crown of the empire."

British rule of India was gentle and stern by turns and was always somewhat patronizing. Great Britain saw India primarily as a source of raw materials to serve the industrial enterprises of England and Scotland, which used Indian raw materials to create manufactured products. India was then used as a market for these new manufactured goods, which were shipped back to India for sale there. The infrastructure of India, including roads, railroads, and telegraph lines, became much more highly developed during the process of British colonization. India cautiously moved down the path of modernization and limited industrialization.

In 1885, the Indian National Congress was formed, essentially to serve as a body for discussing cultural matters. Unlike in the United States, *Congress* in this sense meant purely a discussion society, with no legislative powers whatsoever. It would even have as its president a few years later a British woman, Annie Besant, who was very sympathetic both to India and to Hinduism. Besant was also a prominent figure in the Theosophical Society, an organization founded by the Russian mystic Helena Petrovna Blavatsky, which sought a "secret doctrine" in Hinduism and Buddhism that could be exported to the West. Because the Indian National Congress tended to be dominated by Hindus, the Indian Muslims eventually founded a group of their own called the Muslim League. Once again, the tensions between Hindus and Muslims came to the surface.

The man who succeeded Annie Besant as Indian National Congress president was an English-trained lawyer named Mohandas K. Gandhi. Gandhi had made his reputation fighting the unjust "passbook" laws that restricted the rights of Indians living in South Africa. Now he wanted to apply his skills to help win greater rights for Indians living in India. Eventually, he came to realize that the only way Indians would be able to achieve those rights was by gaining their full independence from Great Britain.

Gandhi then embarked on a campaign to bring about that independence. His methods came to be known as *satyagraha*, "truth-force," which espoused a firm but nonviolent confrontation with the British authorities. Gandhi was beaten and arrested a number of times but remained both committed and nonviolent. Gandhi was given the title *mahatma*, the "great-souled one," or, more simply, "the saint." In the end, thanks in part to his efforts, the British were finally compelled to leave India.

GANDHI ON SATYAGRAHA

Satyagraha is a relentless search for truth and a determination to search truth. . . . Satyagraha has been designed as an effective substitute for violence. . . . Satyagraha is a process of educating public opinion, such that it covers all the elements of the society and makes itself irresistible. . . . The fight of Satyagraha is for the strong in spirit, not the doubter or the timid. Satyagraha teaches us the art of living as well as dying. . . . Satyagraha, of which civil-resistance is but a part, is to me the universal law of life. . . . Satyagraha can rid society of all evils, political, economic, and moral. . . . A genuine Satyagraha should never excite contempt in the opponent even when it fails to command regard or respect. . . . The method of Satyagraha requires that the Satyagrahi should never lose hope, so long as there is the slightest ground left for it. . . . In the dictionary of Satyagraha, there is no enemy. Since Satyagraha is a method of conversion and conviction, it seeks never to use the slightest coercion. . . . In the code of the Satyagrahi, there is no such thing as surrender to brute force.

Source: Quoted from *http://www.carolmoore.net/articles/gandhi-quotes.html*.

After independence, Gandhi had a vision of a greater India that would include both Muslims and Hindus in one society and in which the social divisions of Brahmin, Kshatriya, Vaishya, Shudra, and Untouchable would be seen as a more egalitarian horizontal classification rather than a vertical hierarchy. Gandhi renamed the "Outcastes" the *Harijans*, or "children of God."

The Muslim League, however, insisted on establishing an independent Muslim state, which became known as Pakistan. British India was thus divided between the predominantly Hindu nation-state of India and the mainly Muslim state of Pakistan. This separation came to be known as "the Partition," and the ensuing bloody riots, massacres, and atrocities committed by both Hindus and Muslims rank—save for the two World Wars— among the bloodiest episodes of the twentieth century.

The supreme irony of Gandhi's life was that he was killed not by the British, not even by the Muslims, but by a man associated with a radical branch of Hindu nationalism.

10

Hinduism in the World Today

*Some men cling to the forms of the past and
the memory of the dead, and they live like the dead;
others hurl themselves into foolish novelties until
they plunge into the void; I go forward without losing
my way, for I am always coming back to the most
ancient traditions through a complete revolution,
a total but natural reversal, willed by God and
coming at its appointed time.*

—Mohandas Gandhi

Hinduism has undergone more change in the last two centuries than in all the centuries preceding them. This is largely due first to the impact of Western thought brought by the British Raj (rule) and then by the simple fact of being part of the contemporary process of globalization.

The first attempt at reform of Hinduism is associated with the figure of Rammohan Roy (1772–1833). Rammohan Roy believed that Hinduism had originally been a religion of morality and monotheism but had been subject to much corruption over the centuries. In 1828, he established the *Brahmo Samaj*, "the Assembly of God," in an attempt to reform Hinduism so as to bring out its similarities with the moral norms of Western Christianity. He condemned polytheism, the use of imagery to depict a God beyond all images, superstition, the caste system, and the practice of *sati*—burning widows alive on the funeral pyres of their husbands. Rammohan Roy also began publishing the Vedas in the various spoken languages of India instead of the less accessible Sanskrit.

The Brahmo Samaj did awaken many Hindu thinkers to the need for reforms in Hinduism, but some felt it went too far in trying to accommodate the sensitivities of Western religion. Indeed, Rammohan Roy's successor, Keshub Chander Sen, abandoned Hinduism altogether and became a Christian.

A few decades later, Dayananda Sarasvati (1824–1883) founded the *Arya Samaj*, another reform movement that encouraged Hindus to go "back to the Vedas." In place of the somewhat defensive and apologetic stance that the Brahmo Samaj took toward Christianity, Dayananda Sarasvati asserted the superiority of Vedic religion over the Western religion spread by the missionaries. For Dayananda, the Vedas contained all wisdom and knowledge, including Western science, if one knew how to look for it. In his view, Hindus did not need to feel inferior to Christians.

Nevertheless, like Rammohan Roy, Dayananda also argued that Hinduism had been corrupted over the centuries. He condemned widow-burning as a late and un-Vedic practice.

SRI SRI RAMAKRISHNA KATHAMRITAM ANSWERS QUESTIONS ABOUT THE WAY OF BRAHMO SAMAJ

Question: Sir, what is the way?

Answer: Attachment to God, or, in other words, love for Him. And secondly, prayer.

Q: Which one is the way—love or prayer?

A: First love, and then prayer. . . . And one must always chant the name and glories of God and pray to Him. An old metal pot must be scrubbed every day. What is the use of cleaning it only once? Further, one must practice discrimination and renunciation; one must be conscious of the unreality of the world.

Q: Is it good to renounce the world?

A: Not for all. Those who have not yet come to the end of their enjoyments should not renounce the world. Can one get drunk on two annas' worth of wine?

Q: Then should they lead a worldly life?

A: Yes, they should try to perform their duties in a detached way. Before you break the jack-fruit open, rub your hands with oil, so that the sticky milk will not smear them. The maidservant in a rich man's house performs all her duties, but her mind dwells on her home in the country. This is an example of doing duty in a detached way. You should renounce the world only in mind. But a sunnyasi should renounce the world both inwardly and outwardly.

Source: Available online at *http://www.hinduism.fsnet.co.uk/namoma/kathamritam/ chapter_10/k10_1_Apr_22_1883.htm.*

Animal sacrifice was also a gross misunderstanding of what the Vedic religion was about. The Vedic rituals he advocated were home rituals that offered butter and grain at the new and full moons. The Arya Samaj is still active in India and among overseas Hindus.

The satyagraha campaign of Mohandas Gandhi, better known as "Mahatma" Gandhi, brought about a strong national feeling among Hindus. The campaign also brought to the fore a large number of Western-educated Indian intellectuals who no longer identified themselves with Hinduism at all. They had a much more secular (i.e., nonreligious) view of what India should become. They held that India had succumbed to British colonial power because the nation was backward in the field of modern science. They blamed this backwardness on Hindu attitudes such as those that claimed "the world is illusion" or that the process of change is uncontrollable.

The Indian Constitution called for a secular state, though the exact meaning of this term was somewhat unclear. For the Western-oriented thinkers of India, it meant that the nation would be strictly neutral about religion. For the more traditional, it meant that India would attempt to treat all religions impartially.

Typical of the cultural and religious struggles in India was the question of the role of religion in public education. As in the United States, the issue was how to acknowledge the religious feelings of citizens in a nation that is by constitutional law a secular state. Beginning in 1948, the great modern Indian philosopher Radhakrishnan (1888–1975) headed up a blue-ribbon panel that studied the issue. The committee's members all agreed that education in a secular state must not favor one religion over the others. However, they rejected the idea that such neutrality meant that *no* religion could be taught. Instead, the Radhakrishnan Commission recommended that all religions be taught and honored equally. This recommendation met with opposition from several quarters. Western-educated secularists wanted Indian law to acknowledge that there are many people in the modern world who do not subscribe to any religion. Yet these people also had rights. Christians and Muslims argued that the Radhakrishnan Commission was implicitly assuming that all religions were essentially equal—a very Hindu point of view but one that was not acceptable to Muslims or Christians. The Indian government moved cautiously in the direction of American-style strict neutrality, but there was and is little enthusiasm for such neutrality on matters of religion in local communities, and those who challenge at least cultural religious observances in the schools face social ostracism.

Since Gandhi had renounced all intention of serving in the government of a postindependence India, the first Indian prime minister was Jawaharlal Nehru, one of Gandhi's most prominent followers. Nehru's ideas were somewhat different from Gandhi's, however. Previously, India had always been made up of many different social and political groups and entities. It was precisely this multitude of states that had led to conquest first by the Muslims and then by the British. India at the time of its independence was more united than it had ever been in its history. Forging a unity of all India became the foremost goal on the national political agenda.

Nehru's vision that this unity should be secular was not unchallenged. With Pakistan as a model, various other groups wanted an independent state of their own. For example, the Sikhs, who had been victimized by both Hindus and Muslims in the process of the Partition, wanted an independent state. Dravidian-speaking southern India believed that "Tamilnadu" should be independent from the Hindi-speaking north. This force in Indian politics came to be known as *communalism*, the belief that regional, tribal, or religious loyalty supercedes allegiance to the nation-state of India. The secular vision of India was that, as in the modern West, religion is primarily a private matter and one's foremost loyalty is to one's country.

One particularly difficult problem to deal with was—and still is—the question of caste. The secular constitution of India essentially abolished caste and said that it would have no legal standing. Nonetheless, an Outcaste activist named Babasaheb

(Continued on page 148)

THE SCHEDULED CASTES AND THE SCHEDULED TRIBES (PREVENTION OF ATROCITIES) ACT, 1989

An Act to prevent the commission of offences of atrocities against the members of the Scheduled Castes and the Scheduled Tribes, to provide for Special Courts for the trial of such offences and for the relief and rehabilitation of the victims of such offences and for matters connected therewith or incidental thereto.

Be it enacted by Parliament in the Fortieth Year of the Republic of India as follows:— . . .

3. (1) Whoever, not being a member of a Scheduled Caste or a Scheduled Tribe—

   (i) forces a member of a Scheduled Caste or a Scheduled Tribe to drink or eat any inedible or obnoxious substance;

   (ii) acts with intent to cause injury, insult or annoyance to any member of a Scheduled Caste or a Scheduled Tribe by dumping excreta, waste matter, carcasses or any other obnoxious substance in his premises or neighborhood;

   (iii) forcibly removes clothes from the person of a member of a Scheduled Caste or a Scheduled Tribe or parades him naked or with painted face or body or commits any similar act which is derogatory to human dignity;

   (iv) wrongfully occupies or cultivates any land owned by, or allotted to, or notified by any competent authority to be allotted to, a member of a Scheduled Caste or a Scheduled Tribe or gets the land allotted to him transferred;

   (v) wrongfully dispossesses a member of a Scheduled Caste or a Scheduled Tribe from his land or premises or interferes with the enjoyment of his rights over any land, premises or water;
   . . .

(vii) forces or intimidates a member of a Scheduled Caste or a Scheduled Tribe not to vote or to vote to a particular candidate or to vote in a manner other than that provided by law;

(viii) institutes false, malicious or vexatious suit or criminal or other legal proceedings against a member of a Scheduled Caste or a Scheduled Tribe;

(ix) gives any false or frivolous information to any public servant and thereby causes such public servant to use his lawful power to the injury or annoyance of a member of a Scheduled Caste or Scheduled Tribe;

(x) intentionally insults or intimidates with intent to humiliate a member of a Scheduled Caste or a Scheduled Tribe in any place within public view; . . .

(xiv) denies a member of a Scheduled Caste or a Scheduled Tribe any customary right of passage to a place of public resort or obstructs such member so as to prevent him from using or having access to a place of public resort to which other members of public or any section thereof have a right to use or access to;

(xv) forces or causes a member of a Scheduled Caste or a Scheduled Tribe to leave his house, village or other place of residence;

Shall be punishable with imprisonment for a term, which shall not be less than six months but which may extend to five years and with fine. . . .

(Continued from page 145)

Ambedkar insisted that the question of Untouchability be dealt with in a more proactive fashion. As a result of his efforts, the Indian government set up a program of what in the United States would be called "affirmative action." The government set up specific quotas for how many members of the "scheduled castes" (the Untouchables) must be represented in the Indian Parliament, the civil service, and Indian universities and institutions of higher education. This has, however, had the ironic effect of reinforcing a type of caste-consciousness.

More recently, more politically radical forms of Hinduism have become very influential as a reaction against the previous process of secularization. The nation-building strategy of the radical Hindus is to shape political and social life around the three H's: "Hindu" as the prevailing religion, "Hindi" as the national language (even in the non-Hindi-speaking south), and "Hindustan" as a goal of India embodying Hindu culture and society. More recently, the term *Hindutva*—literally, "Hinduness"—has become the rallying cry of these Hindu nationalists.

HINDUISM OUTSIDE OF INDIA

The British Empire provided an opportunity for many Indian entrepreneurs to try to make their fortunes in other colonies. South Africa, Kenya, and Uganda proved fertile ground for these people, who opened shops and small industries in newly colonized lands in Africa. The entrepreneurs brought with them both their families and their religion. Later, in some parts of Africa, the Indians were driven out when the African colony in which they lived became independent. In South Africa, the Indian community is still very large and politically active. Wherever there is an Indian community, the Hindu religion is acknowledged in some way.

The first sustained contact that Americans had with Hinduism came through the International Parliament of the Religions, held in Chicago in 1893. Swami Vivekananda, representing "the Ramakrishna Mission," attended. Ramakrishna had been a Hindu reformer who had emphasized that, in reality, all religions were one. He identified that oneness of religion with the philosophy of Advaita Vedanta. Vivekananda was bringing Vedanta to the United States much as Western missionaries had brought Christianity to India. From this effort, the Vedanta Society was formed.

While Indian immigrants to the United States have chosen to keep a rather low profile, various movements inspired by Hinduism have become widespread among Americans of non-Indian background. In the 1930s, Swami Paramahansa Yogananda formed the Self-Realization Fellowship, which also had a Vedanta orientation. His book, *Autobiography of a Yogi*, which is filled with stories of miracles and wonders, still remains very popular.

During the so-called "counterculture" movement in the United States in the 1960s, all forms of Asian philosophy and religion became popular. Two movements in particular captured the imagination of spiritual seekers. In 1966, A.C. Bhaktivedanta, also called Swami Prabhupada, founded the International Society for Krishna Consciousness (ISKCON) in New York City. He gathered a number of young Americans around him and taught them devotion to the god Krishna. These people would come to be popularly called "the Hare Krishnas." The members of ISKCON have built several Hindu-style temples in the United States.

Another movement was centered on the Students International Meditation Society, formed by followers of Maharishi Mahesh Yogi. The Maharishi taught a form of mantra meditation called "Transcendental Meditation," which, he argued, brings great psychological benefits regardless of one's religious belief or even lack of belief. Members of the group have gone on to claim that many environmental and social benefits arise when a certain percentage of the population practices meditation. In 1975, Maharishi Mahesh Yogi established a major educational center, Maharishi International University, in Fairfield, Iowa. Clearly, despite its limited origins within India, Hinduism has become a major influence all over the world.

MACAULAY'S MINUTE ON INDIAN EDUCATION

February 2, 1835

A s it seems to be the opinion of some of the gentlemen who compose the committee of Public Instruction, that the course which they have hitherto pursued was strictly prescribed by the British Parliament in 1813, and as, if that opinion be correct, a legislative act will be necessary to warrant a change, I have thought it right to refrain from taking any part in the preparation of the adverse statements which are now before us, and to reserve what I had to say on the subject till it should come before me as a member of the Council of India.

It does not appear to me that the Act of Parliament can, by any art of construction, be made to bear the meaning which has been assigned to it. It contains nothing about the particular languages or sciences which are to be studied. A sum is set apart "for the revival and promotion of literature and the encouragement of the learned natives of India, and for the introduction and promotion of a knowledge of the sciences among the inhabitants of the British territories." It is argued, or rather taken for granted, that by literature, the Parliament can have meant only Arabic and Sanscrit [sic] literature, that they never would have given the honorable appellation of "a learned native" to a native who was familiar with the poetry of Milton, the Metaphysics of Locke, and the Physics of Newton; but that they meant to designate by that name only such persons as might have studied in the sacred books of the Hindoos all the uses of cusa-grass, and all the mysteries of absorption into the Deity. This does not appear to be a very satisfactory interpretation. To take a parallel case; suppose that the Pacha of Egypt, a country once superior in knowledge to the nations of Europe but now sunk far below them, were to appropriate a sum for the purpose of "reviving and promoting literature, and encouraging learned natives of Egypt," would anybody infer that he meant the youth of his pachalic to give years to the study of hieroglyphics, to search into all the doctrines disguised under the fable of Osiris, and to ascertain with all possible accuracy the ritual with which cats and onions were anciently adored? Would he be justly charged with inconsistency, if, instead of employing his young subjects in deciphering obelisks, he were to order them to be instructed in the English and French languages, and in all the sciences to which those languages are the chief keys?

The words on which the supporters of the old system rely do not bear them out, and other words follow which seem to be quite decisive on the other side. This lac of rupees is set apart, not only for "reviving literature in India," the phrase on which their whole interpretation is founded, but also for "the intro-duction and promotion of a knowledge of the sciences among the inhabitants of the British territories,"—words which are alone sufficient to authorise all the changes for which I contend.

If the Council agree in my construction, no legislative Act will be necessary. If they differ from me, I will prepare a short Act rescinding that clause of the Charter of 1813, from which the difficulty arises.

The argument which I have been considering, affects only the form of proceeding. But the admirers of the Oriental system of education have used another argument, which, if we admit it to be valid, is decisive against all change. They conceive that the public faith is pledged to the present system, and that to alter the appropriation of any of the funds which have hitherto been spent in encouraging the study of Arabic and Sanscrit, would be down-right spoliation. It is not easy to understand by what process of reasoning they can have arrived at this conclusion. The grants which are made from the public purse for the encouragement of literature differed in no respect from the grants which are made from the same purse for other objects of real or supposed utility. We found a sanatarium on a spot which we suppose to be healthy. Do we thereby pledge ourselves to keep a sanatarium there, if the result should not answer our expectation? We commence the erection of a pier. Is it a violation of the public faith to stop the works, if we afterwards see reason to believe that the building will be useless? The rights of property are undoubtedly sacred. But nothing endangers those rights so much as the practice, now unhappily too common, of attributing them to things to which they do not belong. Those who would impart to abuses the sanctity of property are in truth imparting to the institution of property the unpopularity and the fragility of abuses. If the Government has given to any person a formal assurance; nay, if the Government has exdted in any person's mind a reasonable expectation that he shall receive a certain income as a teacher or a learner of Sanscrit or Arabic, I would respect that person's pecuniary interests—I would rather err on the side of liberality to individuals than suffer the public faith to be called in question. But to talk of a Government pledging itself to teach certain languages and certain sciences, though those languages may become useless, though those sciences may be exploded, seems to me quite unmeaning. There is not a single word in any public instructions, from which it can be inferred that the Indian Government ever intended to give any pledge on this subject, or ever considered the destination of these funds as unalterably fixed. But had it been otherwise, I should have denied the competence of our predecessors to bind us by any pledge on such a subject. Suppose that a Government had in the last century enacted in the most solemn manner that all its subjects should, to the end of time, be inoculated for the smallpox: would that Government be bound to persist in the practice after Jenner's discovery? These promises, of which nobody claims the performance, and from which nobody can grant a release; these vested rights, which vest in nobody; this property without proprietors; this robbery, which makes nobody poorer, may be comprehended by persons of higher faculties than mine—I consider this plea merely as a set form of words, regularly used both in England and in India, in defence of every abuse for which no other plea can be set up.

I hold this lac [sic] of rupees to be quite at the disposal of the Governor General in Council, for the purpose of promoting learning in India, in any way which may be thought most advisable. I hold his Lordship to be quite as free to direct that it shall no longer be employed in encouraging Arabic and Sanscrit, as he is to direct that the reward for killing tigers in Mysore shall be diminished, that no more public money shall be expended on the chanting at the cathedral.

We now come to the gist of the matter. We have a fund to be employed as Government shall direct for the intellectual improvement of the people of this country. The simple question is, what is the most useful way of employing it?

All parties seem to be agreed on one point, that the dialects commonly spoken among the natives of this part of India, contain neither literary nor scientific information, and are, moreover, so poor and rude that, until they are enriched from some other quarter, it will not be easy to translate any valuable work into them. It seems to be admitted on all sides, that the intellectual improvement of those classes of the people who have the means of pursuing higher studies can at present be effected only by means of some language not vernacular amongst them.

What then shall that language be? One-half of the Committee maintain that it should be the English. The other half strongly recommend the Arabic and Sanscrit. The whole question seems to me to be, which language is the best worth knowing?

I have no knowledge of either Sanscrit or Arabic.—But I have done what I could to form a correct estimate of their value. I have read translations of the most celebrated Arabic and Sanscrit works. I have conversed both here and at home with men distinguished by their proficiency in the Eastern tongues. I am quite ready to take the Oriental learning at the valuation of the Orientalists themselves. I have never found one among them who could deny that a single shelf of a good European library was worth the whole native literature of India and Arabia. The intrinsic superiority of the Western literature is, indeed, fully admitted by those members of the Committee who support the Oriental plan of education.

It will hardly be disputed, I suppose, that the department of literature in which the Eastern writers stand highest is poetry. And I certainly never met with any Orientalist who ventured to maintain that the Arabic and Sanscrit poetry could be compared to that of the great European nations. But when we pass from works of imagination to works in which facts are recorded, and general principles investigated, the superiority of the Europeans becomes absolutely immeasurable. It is, I believe, no exaggeration to say, that all the historical information which has been collected from all the books written in the Sanscrit language is less valuable than what may be found in the most paltry abridgments used at preparatory schools in England. In every branch of physical or moral philosophy, the relative position of the two nations is nearly the same.

How, then, stands the case? We have to educate a people who cannot at present be educated by means of their mother-tongue. We must teach them some foreign language. The claims of our own language it is hardly necessary to recapitulate. It stands pre-eminent even among the languages of the west. It abounds with works of imagination not inferior to the noblest which Greece has bequeathed to us; with models of every species of eloquence; with historical compositions, which, considered merely as narratives, have seldom been surpassed, and which, considered as vehicles of ethical and political instruction, have never been equalled; with just and lively representations of human life and human nature; with the most profound speculations on metaphysics, morals, government, jurisprudence, and trade; with full and correct information respecting every experimental science which tends to preserve the health, to increase the comfort, or to expand the intellect of man. Whoever knows that language has ready access to all the vast intellectual wealth, which all the wisest nations of the earth have created and hoarded in the course of ninety gener-ations. It may safely be said, that the literature now extant in that language is of far greater value than all the literature which three hundred years ago was extant in all the languages of the world together. Nor is this all. In India, English is the language spoken by the ruling class. It is spoken by the higher class of natives at the seats of Government. It is likely to become the language of commerce throughout the seas of the East. It is the language of two great European communities which are rising, the one in the south of Africa, the other in Australasia; communities which are every year becoming more important, and more closely connected with our Indian empire. Whether we look at the intrinsic value of our literature, or at the particular situation of this country, we shall see the strongest reason to think that, of all foreign tongues, the English tongue is that which would be the most useful to our native subjects.

The question now before us is simply whether, when it is in our power to teach this language, we shall teach languages in which, by universal confession, there are no books on any subject which deserve to be compared to our own; whether, when we can teach European science, we shall teach systems which, by universal confession, whenever they differ from those of Europe, differ for the worse; and whether, when we can patronise sound Philosophy and true History, we shall countenance, at the public expense, medical doctrines, which would disgrace an English farrier,—Astronomy, which would move laughter in girls at an English boarding school,—History, abounding with kings thirty feet high, and reigns thirty thousand years long,—and Geography, made up of seas of treacle and seas of butter.

We are not without experience to guide us. History furnishes several analogous cases, and they all teach the same lesson. There are in modern times, to go no further, two memorable instances of a great impulse given to the mind of a whole society,—of prejudices overthrown,—of knowledge diffused,—taste purified,—of arts and sciences planted in countries which had recently been ignorant and barbarous.

The first instance to which I refer, is the great revival of letters among the Western nations at the close of the fifteenth and the beginning of the sixteenth century. At that time almost every thing that was worth reading was contained in the writings of the ancient Greeks and Romans. Had our ancestors acted as the Committee of Public Instruction has hitherto acted; had they neglected the language of Cicero and Tacitus; had they confined their attention to the old dialects of our own island; had they printed nothing and taught nothing at the universities but Chronicles in Anglo-Saxon, and Romances in Norman-French, would England have been what she now is? What the Greek and Latin were to the contemporaries of More and Ascham, our tongue is to the people of India. The literature of England is now more valuable than that of classical antiquity. I doubt whether the Sanscrit literature be as valuable as that of our Saxon and Norman progenitors. In some departments,—in History, for example, I am certain that it is much less so.

Another instance may be said to be still before our eyes. Within the last hundred and twenty years, a nation which has previously been in a state as barbarous as that in which our ancestors were before the crusades, has gradually emerged from the ignorance in which it was sunk, and has taken its place among civilized communities.—I speak of Russia. There is now in that country a large educated class, abounding with persons fit to serve the state in the highest functions, and in no wise inferior to the most accomplished men who adorn the best circles of Paris and London. There is reason to hope that this vast empire, which in the time of our grandfathers was probably behind the Punjab, may, in the time of our grandchildren, be pressing close on France and Britain in the career of improvement. And how was this change effected? Not by flattering national prejudices: not by feeding the mind of the young Muscovite with the old women's stories which his rude fathers had believed: not by filling his head with lying legends about St. Nicholas: not by encouraging him to study the great question, whether the world was or was not created on the 13th of September: not by calling him "a learned native," when he has mastered all these points of knowledge: but by teaching him those foreign languages in which the greatest mass of information had been laid up, and thus putting all that information within his reach. The languages of Western Europe civilized Russia. I cannot doubt that they will do for the Hindoo what they have done for the Tartar.

And what are the arguments against that course which seems to be alike recommended by theory and by experience? It is said that we ought to secure the cooperation of the native public, and that we can do this only by teaching Sanscrit and Arabic.

I can by no means admit that when a nation of high intellectual attainments undertakes to Superintend the education of a nation comparatively ignorant, the learners are absolutely to prescribe the course which is to be taken by the teachers. It is not necessary, however, to say any thing on this subject. For it is proved by unanswerable evidence that we are not at present securing the Cooperation of the natives. It would be bad enough to consult their intellectual taste at the expense of their intellectual health. But we are consulting neither,—we are withholding from them the learning for which they are craving, we are forcing on them the mock-learning which they nauseate.

This is proved by the fact that we are forced to pay our Arabic and Sanscrit students, while those who learn English are willing to pay us. All the declamations in the world about the love and reverence of the natives for their sacred dialects will never, in the mind of any impartial person, outweigh the undisputed fact, that we cannot find, in all our vast empire, a single student who will let us teach him those dialects unless we will pay him.

I have now before me the accounts of the Madrassa for one month,—in the month of December, 1833. The Arabic students appear to have been seventy-seven in number. All receive stipends from the public. The whole amount paid to them is above 500 rupees a month. On the other side of the account stands the following item: Deduct amount realized from the out-students of English for the months of May, June and July last, 103 rupees.

I have been told that it is merely from want of local experience that I am surprised at these phenomena, and that it is not the fashion for students in India to study at their own charges. This only confirms me in my opinion. Nothing is more certain than that it never can in any part of the world be necessary to pay men for doing what they think pleasant and profitable. India is no exception to this rule. The people of India do not require to be paid for eating rice when they are hungry, or for wearing woollen cloth in the cold season. To come nearer to the case before us, the children who learn their letters and a little elementary Arithmetic from the village school-master are not paid by him. He is paid for teaching them. Why then is it necessary to pay people to learn

Sanscrit and Arabic? Evidently because it is universally felt that the Sanscrit and Arabic are languages, the knowledge of which does not compensate for the trouble of acquiring them. On all such subjects the state of the market is the decisive test.

Other evidence is not wanting, if other evidence were required. A petition was presented last year to the Committee by several ex-students of the Sanscrit College. The petitioners stated that they had studied in the college ten or twelve years; that they had made themselves acquainted with Hindoo literature and science; that they had received certificates of proficiency: and what is the fruit of all this! "Notwithstanding such testimonials," they say, "we have but little prospect of bettering our condition without the kind assistance of your Honorable Committee, the indifference with which we are generally looked upon by our countrymen leaving no hope of encouragement and assistance from them." They therefore beg that they may be recommended to the Governor General for places under the Government, not places of high dignity or emolument, but such as may just enable them to exist. "We want means," they say, "for a decent living, and for our progressive improvement, which, however, we cannot obtain without the assistance of Government, by whom we have been educated and maintained from childhood." They conclude by representing, very pathetically, that they are sure that it was never the intention of Government, after behaving so liberally to them during their education, to abandon them to destitution and neglect.

I have been used to see petitions to Government for compensation. All these petitions, even the most unreasonable of them, proceeded on the supposition that some loss had been sustained— that some wrong had been inflicted. These are surely the first petitioners who ever demanded compensation for having been educated gratis, for having been supported by the public during twelve years, and then sent forth into the world well furnished with literature and science. They represent their education as an injury which gives them a claim on the Government for redress, as an injury for which the stipends paid to them during the infliction were a very inadequate compensation. And I doubt not that they are in the right. They have wasted the best years of life in learning what procures for them neither bread nor respect. Surely we might, with advantage, have saved the cost of making these persons useless and miserable; surely, men may be brought up to be burdens to the public and objects of contempt to their neighbours at a somewhat smaller charge to the state. But such is our policy. We do not even stand neuter in the contest between truth and falsehood. We are not content to leave the natives to the influence of their own hereditary prejudices. To the natural difficulties which obstruct the progress of sound science in the East, we add fresh difficulties of our own making. Bounties and premiums, such as ought not to be given even for the propagation of truth, we lavish on false taste and false philosophy.

By acting thus we create the very evil which we fear. We are making that opposition which we do not find. What we spend on the Arabic and Sanscrit colleges is not merely a dead loss to the cause of truth; it is bounty-money paid to raise up champions of error. It goes to form a nest, not merely of helpless place-hunters, but of bigots prompted alike by passion and by interest to raise a cry against every useful scheme of education. If there should be any opposition among the natives to the change which I recommend, that opposition will be the effect of our own system. It will be headed by persons supported by our stipends and trained in our colleges. The longer we persevere in our present course, the more formidable will that opposition be. It will be every year reinforced by recruits whom we are paying. From the native society left to itself, we have no difficulties to apprehend; all the murmuring will come from that oriental interest which we have, by artificial means, called into being, and nursed into strength.

There is yet another fact, which is alone sufficient to prove that the feeling of the native public, when left to itself, is not such as the supporters of the old system represent it to be. The Committee have thought fit to lay out above a lac of rupees in printing Arabic and Sanscrit books. Those books find no purchasers. It is very rarely that a single copy is disposed of. Twenty-three thousand volumes, most of them folios and quartos, fill the libraries, or rather the lumber-rooms, of this body. The Committee contrive to get rid of some portion of their vast stock of oriental literature by giving books away. But they cannot give so fast as they print. About twenty thousand rupees a year are spent in adding fresh masses of waste paper to a hoard which, I should think, is already sufficiently ample. During the last three years, about sixty thousand rupees have been expended in this manner. The sale of Arabic and Sanscrit books, during those three years, has not yielded quite one thousand rupees. In the mean time the School-book Society is selling seven or eight thousand English volumes every year, and not only pays the expenses of printing, but realises a profit of 20 per cent on its outlay.

The fact that the Hindoo law is to be learned chiefly from Sanscrit books, and the Mahomedan law from Arabic books, has been much insisted on, but seems not to bear at all on the question. We are commanded by Parliament to ascertam and digest the laws of India. The assistance of a law Commission has been given to us for that purpose. As soon as the code is promulgated, the Shasster and the Hedaya will be useless to a Moonsiff or Sudder Ameen. I hope and trust that before the boys who are now entering at the Madrassa and the Sanscrit college have completed their studies, this great work will be finished. It would be manifestly absurd to educate the rising generation with a view to a state of things which we mean to alter before they reach manhood.

But there is yet another argument which seems even more untenable. It is said that the Sanscrit and Arabic are the languages in which the sacred books of a hundred millions of people are written, and that they are, on that account, entitled to peculiar encouragement. Assuredly it is the duty of the British Government in India to be not only tolerant, but neutral on all religious questions. But to encourage the study of a literature admitted to be of small intrinsic value, only because that literature inculcates the most serious errors on the most important subjects, is a course hardly reconcileable with reason, with morality, or even with that very neutrality which ought, as we all agree, to be sacredly preserved. It is confessed that a language is barren of useful knowledge. We are to teach it because it is fruitful of monstrous superstitions. We are to teach false History, false Astronomy, false Medicine, because we find them in company with a false religion. We abstain, and I trust shall always abstain, from giving any public encouragement to those who are engaged in the work of converting natives to Christianity. And while we act thus, can we reasonably and decently bribe men out of the revenues of the state to waste their youth in learning how they are to purify themselves after touching an ass, or what text of the Vedas they are to repeat to expiate the crime of killing a goat?

It is taken for granted by the advocates of Oriental learning, that no native of this country can possibly attain more than a mere smattering of English. They do not attempt to prove this; but they perpetually insinuate it. They designate the education which their opponents recommend as a mere spelling book education. They assume it as undeniable, that the question is between a profound knowledge of Hindoo and Arabian literature and science on the one side, and a superficial knowledge of the rudiments of English on the other. This is not merely an assumption, but an assumption contrary to all reason and experience. We know that foreigners of all nations do learn our language sufficiently to have access to all the most abstruse knowledge which it contains, sufficiently to relish even the more delicate graces of our most idiomatic writers. There are in this very town natives who are quite competent to discuss political or scientific questions with fluency and precision in the English language. I have heard the gentlemen with a liberality and an intelligence which would do credit to any member of the Committee of Public Instruction. Indeed it is unusual to find, even in the literary circles of the continent, any foreigner who can express himself in English with so much facility and correctness as we find in many Hindoos. Nobody, I suppose, will contend that English is so difficult to a Hindoo as Greek to an Englishman. Yet an intelligent English youth, in a much smaller number of years than our unfortunate pupils pass at the Sanscrit college, becomes able to read, to enjoy, and even to imitate, not unhappily, the compositions of the best Greek

Authors. Less than half the time which enables an English youth to read Herodotus and Sophocles, ought to enable a Hindoo to read Hume and Milton.

To sum up what I have said, I think it clear that we are not fettered by the Act of Parliament of 1813; that we are not fettered by any pledge expressed or implied; that we are free to employ our finds as we choose; that we ought to employ them in teaching what is best worth knowing; that English is better worth knowing than Sanscrit or Arabic; that the natives are desirous to be taught English, and are not desirous to be taught Sanscrit or Arabic; that neither as the languages of law, nor as the languages of religion, have the Sanscrit and Arabic any peculiar claim to our engagement; that it is possible to make natives of this country thoroughly good English scholars, and that to this end our efforts ought to be directed.

In one point I fully agree with the gentlemen to whose general views I am opposed. I feel with them, that it is impossible for us, with our limited means, to attempt to educate the body of the people. We must at present do our best to form a class who may be interpreters between us and the millions whom we govern; a class of persons, Indian in blood and colour, but English in taste, in opinions, in morals, and in intellect. To that class we may leave it to refine the vernacular dialects of the country, to enrich those dialects with terms of science borrowed from the Western nomenclature, and to render them by degrees fit vehicles for conveying knowledge to the great mass of the population.

I would strictly respect all existing interests. I would deal even generously with all individuals who have had fair reason to expect a pecuniary provision. But I would strike at the root of the bad system which has hitherto been fostered by us. I would at once stop the printing of Arabic and Sanscrit books, I would abolish the Madrassa and the Sanscrit college at Calcutta. Benares is the great seat of Brahmanical learning; Delhi, of Arabic learning. If we retain the Sanscrit college at Benares and the Mahometan college at Delhi, we do enough, and much more than enough in my opinion, for the Eastern languages. If the

Benares and Delhi colleges should be retained, I would at least recommend that no stipends shall be given to any students who may hereafter repair thither, but that the people shall be left to make their own choice between the rival systems of education without being bribed by us to learn what they have no desire to know. The funds which would thus be placed at our disposal would enable us to give larger encouragement to the Hindoo college at Calcutta, and to establish in the principal cities throughout the Presidencies of Fort William and Agra schools in which the English language might be well and thoroughly taught.

If the decision of his Lordship in Council should be such as I anticipate, I shall enter on the performance of my duties with the greatest zeal and alacrity. If, on the other hand, it be the opinion of the Government that the present system ought to remain unchanged, I beg that I may be permitted to retire from the chair of the Committee. I feel that I could not be of the smallest use there—I feel, also, that I should be lending my countenance to what I firmly believe to be a mere delusion. I believe that the present system tends, not to accelerate the progress of truth, but to delay the natural death of expiring errors. I conceive that we have at present no right to the respectable name of a Board of Public Instruction. We are a Board for wasting public money, for printing books which are of less value than the paper on which they are printed was while it was blank; for giving artificial encouragement to absurd history, absurd metaphysics, absurd physics, absurd theology; for raising up a breed of scholars who find their scholarship an encumbrance and a blemish, who live on the public while they are receiving their education, and whose education is so utterly useless to them that when they have received it they must either starve or live on the public all the rest of their lives. Entertaining these opinions, I am naturally desirous to decline all share in the responsibility of a body, which unless it alters its whole mode of proceeding, I must consider not merely as useless, but as positively noxious.

The following is an overview of the historical development of Hinduism. Precise dating is difficult until about A.D. 1200 when the Muslims entered India and began to keep more detailed historical records. This chronology is arranged by centuries, with more precise dates given where available.

3000–1750 B.C.	Indus Valley Civilization
1500 B.C.	Indo-Aryan migrations into India
1400–800 B.C.	Vedic Samhitas and Vedic ritual literature take form
800–600 B.C.	Forest Treatises and the early Upanishads developed
600–400 B.C.	Major Upanishads are composed; cities, writing, and coinage emerge

c. 1100
Muslim Sufis enter India

c. 1500 B.C.
Indo-Aryans
migrate to India

c. 1000
Tantric religion becomes
part of Hinduism

c. 600
Vedanta school established

1500   500   BC AD   500   1500

c. A.D. 200
Bhagavad Gita
finalized

1206
Muslim sultanate
established at Delhi

326 B.C.
Alexander the Great
invades Indus Valley

1498
Vasco da Gama visits India

500 – 400 B.C. Earliest references to devotional religion

400 – 300 B.C. Classical form of Sanskrit language takes form (earliest versions of the epics); early Hinduism spreads through North India; major philosophical schools begin to develop

326 B.C. Alexander the Great invades the Indus Valley during his last major campaign; kingdoms combining Greek and Indian culture flourish for several centuries

272 B.C. Great Mauryan emperor, Ashoka, ascends the throne, favors Buddhism, and makes it a major religion in northern India

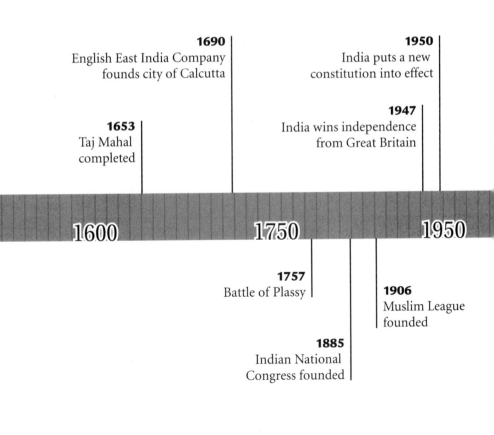

1690
English East India Company
founds city of Calcutta

1950
India puts a new
constitution into effect

1653
Taj Mahal
completed

1947
India wins independence
from Great Britain

1600   1750   1950

1757
Battle of Plassy

1906
Muslim League
founded

1885
Indian National
Congress founded

CHRONOLOGY

200–100 B.C.	Dharma-sastra texts on law and social organization begin to take shape; devotional religion becomes more widespread; earliest form of Bhagavad Gita is composed; although it is a part of the larger Mahabharata, it circulates independently as a source of spiritual inspiration
A.D. 200–300	Final form of the Bhagavad Gita is established; Yoga Sutras are composed by Patanjali
300–400	Classical temple-building begins; Puranas, popular Hindu devotional texts, begin to take present form
500–600	The Tantric religious movement begins to take form, drawing upon earlier elements of goddess worship and shamanistic religious practices that had become prominent in Bengal in eastern India
600–700	Vedanta philosophical school is established, taking its basic ideas from the Upanishads
700–800	Hindu devotional religion (*bhakti*) begins to take more definite form, particularly in Tamil-speaking southern India; devotional movement is strengthened by Alvars, chiefly Nammalvar, who are devoted to Vishnu; Vedanta philosophy grows and spreads through northern India; separate philosophical school, the Mimamsa, develops
800–900	Great philosopher Shankara, often called Shankaracarya, "the teacher Shankara," brings the Advaita Vedanta philosophy to its intellectual height
900–1000	Vaishnavite Bhagavata Purana is composed; the period of the devotional poets, Alvars and Nayanars, ends

1000–1100 Tantric religion finds a home in Hinduism, particularly in the Shaivite tradition and Shaktism

1100–1200 Muslim Sufi orders enter India, seeking converts to Islam

1175 Great bhakti poet Jayadeva flourishes

1206 Muslim sultanate established at Delhi; Muslims begin to play an increasingly important role in Indian history

1450–1547 Life of Mirabai, great female bhakti poet

1483–1530 Life of Babur, founder of Mughal Empire

1483–1563 Life of Surdas, great devotee of Krishna

1486–1533 Life of Chaitanya, great Bengali bhakti leader

1498 Vasco da Gama of Portugal visits India, beginning Western contact with India

1500 Francis Xavier brings Jesuits to India

1518 Death of great poet Kabir

1543–1623 Life of Tulsidas, the North Indian bhakti poet

1556–1605 Reign of Akbar, the most tolerant of the Mughal emperors

1757 Battle of Plassy: British/Indian forces defeat French colonial forces; India gains exposure to Western ideas, Europeans become more aware of Indian religion and philosophy

1828 Hindu reformer Rammohan Roy (1772–1833) establishes Brahmo Samaj, an attempt to reform Hinduism to emphasize similarities with moral norms of Western Christianity

1835 The "Macaulay Minute" issued, recommending that English-style education be introduced into India

1857–1858 Sepoy Mutiny (First War of Independence) takes place; Mughal Empire is abolished and Great Britain takes direct control of India

1875 Dayananda Saravati (1824–1883) founds the Arya Samaj, another reform movement encouraging Hindus to go "back to the Vedas"; Madame Helena Petrovna Blavatsky and Colonel Henry Steele Olcott form Theosophical Society

1885 Indian National Congress founded

1886 Death of Shri Ramakrishna, Hindu reformer

1893 Vivekananda, a disciple of Ramakrishna, attends World Parliament of Religions in Chicago

1897 Vivekananda establishes the Ramakrishna Mission, spreading Vedanta ideas in Europe and United States; Vedanta Society formed

1906 Muslim League founded

1914 Shri Aurobindo (1872–1950) establishes *ashram* (religious settlement) at Pondicherry (later becomes spiritual center called Auroville)

1920 Mohandas Gandhi begins movement for independence from Great Britain

1947 India gains independence from Great Britain; Muslim League establishes independent Muslim state of Pakistan

1948 Gandhi assassinated by Hindu extremist

1950   India establishes constitution, is declared a
        secular state, and caste distinctions are deprived
        of legal status

1966   A.C. Bhaktivedanta, also called Swami Prabhupada,
        founds International Society for Krishna Conscious-
        ness in New York City

1975   Maharishi Mahesh Yogi establishes Maharishi
        International University in Fairfield, Iowa

1992   Hindu militants destroy sixteenth-century Muslim
        mosque at Adyodha, a defining episode in Hindu-
        Muslim relations

NOTES

Chapter 1:
Introduction to Hinduism

1 *The New York Public Library Desk Reference*, 4th ed., New York: A Stonesong Press Book, 2002, p. 288.

2 Available online at http://www.pluralism.org.

Chapter 2:
Foundations of Hinduism

3 David S. Noss, "The Religion of the Vedic Age," *A History of the World's Religions*, 11th ed. Upper Saddle River, NJ: Prentice Hall, 2003, p. 83.

4 The four varna (Brahmin, Kshatriya, Vaishya, and Shudra) are "castes" or "social classes."

5 See, e.g., Edwin F. Bryant, *The Quest for the Origins of Vedic Culture*. New York: Oxford University Press, 2001.

Chapter 3:
Sacred Scriptures in Hinduism

6 *Bhagavad Gita: The Song of God*, trans. Prabhavananda and Christopher Isherwood, New York: Merton Books, 1951, pp. 38, 39.

Chapter 4:
Worldview of Hinduism

7 Brahma has no temples dedicated to his honor in India, but he is a very popular deity in Thailand. Equally intriguing is the fact that Brahma's wife, Saraswati, Goddess of learning and the arts, is very popular in India and has many temples devoted to her.

8 The Hindu deities have animals associated with them, which are called their "vehicles," and they are often portrayed riding on their animal vehicles.

9 Bhagavad Gita, Chapter 4, Verses 7–8, quoted online at http://www.ashram.org/html/chapter4.htm.

10 Actually, Shaivism was the predominant form of devotion for the first millennium of the common era (ca. 1–1000 A.D.), and

Vaishnavism was second in importance. After ca. 1000 A.D., Vaishnavism became more prevalent than Shaivism.

Chapter 6:
Growing Up Hindu

11 S. Radhakrishnan, *Religion and Society*, London: George, Allen and Unwin Ltd., 1966, p. 171.

12 "Arjuna's Advice to Krishna from the Bhagavad Gita," available online at http://www.globaled.org/curriculum/globalSystems8.html.

Chapter 8:
Hindu Holidays

13 The author is particularly indebted to Elizabeth Breuilly et al., *Religions of the World*, Facts on File, 1999, for the outline and general principles of these holidays.

14 The author wishes to thank Ann Marie Bahr and the *Brookings Register* for permission to incorporate sections of her newspaper column into this chapter on Hindu holidays.

15 Hindu images often have multiple arms, hands, and faces, indicating their many powers. Sarasvati is typically portrayed with four arms.

16 From the vantage point of American culture, where a phallus is never displayed publicly except as an obscene gesture, it is difficult to comprehend the reverence Hindus have for this symbol. The phallus of God is not a subject for locker-room humor in India. It is an object of profound respect because it represents the source of life itself.

Chapter 9:
Memories

17 *The Chronicle of Higher Education*, January 23, 2004, p. A41.

18 "Colonialism: Macauley's Minute," *Hinduism Today*, available online at http://www.hinduismtoday.com/archives/2000/9-10/2000-9-20.shtml.

GLOSSARY AND NOTES ON THE SANSKRIT LANGUAGE

Sanskrit (the "perfect" or "completed" language) is one of the oldest known forms in the Indo-European family of languages. It is related to Latin, Greek, German, and, ultimately, to English.

Sanskrit, the preeminent philosophical and literary language in classical India, may not be spoken on the streets, but it is by no means a dead language. Poems, plays, and essays are still written in Sanskrit. All-India Radio broadcasts regular programs in Sanskrit, and academics have delivered scholarly papers in the language.

Sanskrit is written in a script called *Devanagari*, the script of "the city of the gods." Indian expertise in linguistics made this script into one of the most accurate renditions of sounds of any living alphabet. There are about fifty letters in Devanagari. To render them in Roman letters, diacritical marks are often used to distinguish one letter from another.

Despite their apparent length, Sanskrit words are very easy to pronounce: they are pronounced the way they are spelled, and they are spelled the way they are pronounced. Vowels are pronounced in the "Italian" style: "a" as in "f*a*ther," "e" as in "ob*e*y," "i" as in "mach*i*ne," "o" as in "*o*wn," and "u" as in "m*oo*n." The "c" represents the English "*ch*" sound, never a "*k*" sound. For example, *vac* is pronounced "*vahch.*"

Advaita—"Non-dual"; the name of an important school of Vedanta, particularly associated with the great Hindu philosopher Sankaracarya.

ahimsa—Nonviolence; an honored virtue in classical Indian texts and an important element of Gandhi's satyagraha campaign.

apsaras—Female heavenly attendants in the spiritual realms of the devas.

asura—A demonic being, enemy of the devas.

atman—The True Self; the most profound level of the human spirit, which is of the same nature as Brahman, the Infinite Spirit of the universe.

avatar—"Descent"; an incarnation of deity, particularly Vishnu, into some physical form to fight demons, restore order, and instruct the world. Traditionally, there are ten; Rama and Krishna are the most popular. The word is sometimes broadened in modern usage to mean any of the great religious teachers of the world, such as Jesus or Muhammad.

bhakti—The religious devotion and overwhelming love given to a particular Hindu god—such as Shiva, the Goddess, Krishna, or Rama. It is the most widespread form of religious expression in India.

Brahman—The underlying supreme spirit of the universe, possessing being, consciousness, and blissfulness to an infinite extent. The Hindu name for the highest divine beyond all categories and limitations such as form and personality, and which can only be referred to as "that One" (*tad ekam*).

Brahmin—Name given to the highest priestly set of castes; the social class from which Hindu priests and religious teachers are drawn.

caste—See *jati*.

communalism—The idea that loyalty to one's own local community or to one's fellow religionists should supercede loyalty to the modern nation-state of India.

devas—Literally, "the shining ones"; they are the great divine beings of the ancient Vedic religion, many of whom are still worshiped and given honor today.

dharma—The natural unchanging laws that govern the universe and human life; generally translated as "law" or "duty," but no one English word can fully encompass its meaning. In the realm of nature, it means the "law of nature," which guides everything. In the realm of knowledge, it means "truth." In the realm of ethics, it means "righteousness." In society, it means "justice," but that came to mean "the structure of the caste system." Then, by extension, it came to mean one's "duty in the caste system," which is probably the first thing a contemporary Hindu would think of when hearing the word.

Dharma-shastra—A textbook on dharma written in the days of early classical India describing how a Hindu community should be structured, what duties are expected of each person, and how each individual life should be lived; remains an important resource for Hinduism even in the present day.

ethnocentric—Intended for a particular set of persons and for a particular culture, and not for people outside that culture. Hinduism is an example of an ethnocentric religion. On the other hand, religions such as Christianity and Islam are universal; they are intended for everybody in the world.

Ganges—The sacred river of India, running across the top third of the Indian subcontinent. Bathing in the Ganges River is said to spiritually purify a person; those who wish to be cremated when they die often request that their ashes be thrown into the Ganges.

gopis—"Cowgirls"; young women who tend the cattle at pasture and who form the image of the devotee of Krishna.

guru—A spiritual teacher in Hinduism; someone who instructs in Hindu doctrines and practices; the guru-student relationship is very important, and a student is expected to give great care and devotion to his teacher.

Indus Valley civilization—An ancient civilization that flourished along the Indus River in northwestern India; the connection of this civilization to the incoming Indo-Aryans is still disputed.

jati—Usually translated as a "caste," which is actually a term from Portuguese. It is a social grouping defined by birth: One is born in a specific jati, expected to marry in that jati, and expected to perform the social duties and occupations associated with that jati.

jiva—Soul; that part of the total person, along with the atman, that transmigrates from one body to another.

jnana yoga—A form of yoga that centers on gaining direct knowledge of reality.

karma—The accumulated effect of actions in this and previous lives; the moral law of cause and effect; the mechanism that determines the quality of one's life both now and in future rebirths.

karma yoga—The spiritual discipline that centers on one's actions in the world, performed in a spiritual way or with a spiritual consciousness. This can include but is not limited to performance of certain rituals, ethical living, or using the acts of one's daily life as a focus for meditation.

Kshatriyas—The second-highest varna in the caste system; the warrior class.

lingam—The Sanskrit word for the male generative organ, often used as a symbol of the god Shiva; the corresponding female organ is called a *yoni* and also figures in Shaivite worship.

mantra—Words of power repeated in worship or in meditation that, when recited inwardly, become a focus for mental attention. They can be specific prayers but they can also be simply a series of syllables deemed to have power of their own.

Maya—A word describing the world around us as merely dependent existence or existence projected from Brahman or Infinite Spirit. It sometimes has the connotation of "illusion."

moksha—"Release"; in particular, release from reincarnation, the cycle of rebirth and death caused by karma. Different Hindu groups define moksha in somewhat different ways, much as different Christian groups define "salvation" in different ways. In the monistic Hinduism, moksha is most often used to mean the achievement of full conscious unity with Ultimate Reality, Brahman. In devotional Hinduism, moksha refers to eternal personal existence in a paradise in the full presence of God.

monism—A particular type of religion that says that the highest divine reality is above and beyond all designations and yet completely pervades and undergirds both natural and human existence.

OM (sometimes spelled *AUM*)—The supreme sound, the infinite syllable from which all creation arises.

polytheism—A particular type of religion in which there are many gods, goddesses, or divine beings, each of which has its own particular place and function in the religious cosmos and each of which is worthy of respect and worship in some way.

puja—An act of worship or devotion paid either to a god or to one's ancestors.

reincarnation—The belief that when a person dies (or indeed when any living being dies), the soul of that individual will be reborn in another body; this process will continue life after life until that individual achieves *moksha*, or "release."

Rig Veda—The most basic and most important of the four Vedas. It dates from about 1400 B.C. and consists of 1,028 hymns in ten books.

rishi—Literally, a "seer"; a holy man, particularly the class of holy men who are said to have "seen" the eternal Vedas and then embodied their visions in poetic hymns that form the first part of the Vedic scripture.

sadhu—A Hindu holy man, much the same as a *sunnyasi*, or "renunciate."

samadhi—Superconsciousness; a state of expanded consciousness as a result of meditation; one of a number of levels of awareness, the highest being full enlightenment or the mystical union.

Samhitas—The most ancient part of the Vedas; collections of hymns honoring the Vedic gods, the devas.

samsara—The endless round of reincarnation, births, and deaths; sometimes used more generally to describe the entire impermanent world.

samskara—A Hindu ritual connected with transitional life stages; what are often called "rites of passage."

Sanatana Dharma—The "everlasting Law"; a term Hindus use to describe their own religion.

sannyasin—A man who has renounced all attachment to the world, even caste and family, to devote himself to seeking the divine; sunnyasis live on the generosity of others (it is regarded as a very worthy act to give to a sunnyasi) and are sworn to strict celibacy.

sati (sometimes spelled *suttee*)—The practice of burning a widow on the cremation fire of her dead husband. The practice has been outlawed in contemporary India.

Shaiva or **Shaivite**—A devotee of Shiva.

Shakta—A devotee of the goddess Shakti, the wife of Shiva, following the forms of worship described in the Hindu Tantras.

Shudra—The servant class; the lowest of the traditional four varnas of the caste system.

soma—A sacred drink consumed by certain members of the ancient Vedic society that is said to bring about greatly heightened consciousness and to bring one directly to the gods. Various Western scholars believe that the soma may have been made from some form of psychotropic plant.

theism—A type of religion in which mainly one god is worshiped, though without necessarily denying that other subordinate gods and goddesses may exist; the principal god is personal in nature and relates to the worshiper in a person-to-person way.

tripartite ideology—The theory that the ancient Indo-European-speaking peoples had three main social classes: priests, warriors, and commoners.

upanayana—The ceremony bestowing the sacred thread on young men of the upper three varnas.

Upanishads—The last phase of Vedic sacred scripture and the texts that have most directly shaped the later development of Hinduism.

Vaishnava or Vaishnavite—A worshiper of Vishnu or of any of his avatars or incarnations, such as Rama or Krishna.

Vaishyas—The commoner class in Vedic times; the class that includes both agricultural and merchant castes.

Varanasi—A city that is sacred to Hindus and where many come to bathe in the Ganges River to be purified; the city is better known in the West as Benares.

varnas—The broad social divisions and groupings of the caste system. There are four varnas: the Brahmins, the Kshatriyas, the Vaishyas, and the Shudras; the Untouchables are often considered something like a fifth varna. The varnas are ways of grouping and classifying the many jatis or castes that exist in India.

Vedas—The great body of sacred scripture that makes up the foundation of Hinduism. The full range of Vedic literature includes the archaic hymns, the Samhitas, the ritual texts, a group of meditative texts written "out in the forest," and the Upanishads, probably the most influential of all the Vedic scriptures. When Western scholars talk about the "Vedas," they are often thinking primarily of the hymns, but when Indians hear "Vedas," they think first of the Upanishads.

yoga—A spiritual discipline involving mind or body or both; a method of meditation or spiritual discipline to achieve a higher state of consciousness. Different forms of yoga exist, including the yoga of knowledge (*jnana yoga*) and the yoga of action (*karma yoga*); even bhakti or devotion is sometimes considered a form of yoga.

It is difficult for a teacher of world religion courses to list all the books from which a knowledge of Hinduism has been derived. Nevertheless, the works listed here have been particularly helpful in the writing of this book.

For the outline of the Hindu holidays, the following deserves special acknowledgment: Elizabeth Breuilly, et al., *Religions of the World* (Facts on File Inc., 1997). This treatment of holidays was supplemented by articles on holidays written by Professor Ann Marie B. Bahr for the *Brookings Register* in South Dakota. The Breuilly book was also very helpful in the development of material about the Hindu temple.

Bahr, Ann Marie. "Hindus Celebrate Janmashtami." The *Brookings Register* (2 September 1999), p. A7.

Basham, Arthur. *The Wonder That Was India.* New York: Grove Press, 1966.

Batchelor, Anthony. "The Hindu Temple." Available online at http://www.templenet.com/Articles/hintemp.html.

"Bharat Natyam." Available online at www.indiansaga.info/art/bharatnatyam_dance.html.

Breuilly, Elizabeth, Joanne O'Brien, and Martin Palmer. *Religions of the World.* Facts on File, Inc., 1997.

Bryant, Edwin. *The Quest for the Origins of Vedic Culture.* New York: Oxford University Press, 2001.

Courtney, David, Ph.D. "Introduction to North Indian Music." Available online at *www.chandrakantha.com*/articles/Indian_music/.

Devi, Ragini. "Hindu Conception of Music." Available online at *www.geocities.com/Athens/Academy/* 5185/1-6music.html.

Du Bary, Theodore, et al. *Sources of the Indian Tradition.* New York: Columbia University Press, 1966.

Elder, Joseph, ed. *Lectures in Indian Civilization.* Dubuque, Iowa: Kendall/Hunt Publishing, 1970.

"Hinduism." Available online at *www.vegetarian-restaurants.net/ OtherInfo/Hindu.htm.*

"Hindu Music." Available online at *http://reference.allrefer.com/ encyclopedia/H/Hindumus.html.*

Hopkins, Thomas. *The Hindu Religious Tradition.* Belmont, Calif.: Dickenson Publishing Co., 1971.

Kamat, K.L. "Dances of India" at *www.kamat.com/kalranga/dances/dances.htm*

———. "Gatekeeper in Indian Art." Available online at http://www.kamat.com/kalranga/dwar/dwar.htm.

———. "The Sun Temple at Konark." Available online at http://www.kamat.com/kalranga/nindia/orissa/konaark.htm.

"Kathak." Available online at *www.indiansaga.info/art/kathak_dance.html.*

"Kathakali." Available online at *www.indiansaga.info/art/kathakali_dance.html.*

Knipe, David M. *Hinduism.* San Francisco: Harper, 1991.

"Konark." Available online at http://www.cisce.org/india/destinations/konark.htm.

"Konark Sun Temple." Available online at http://www.taj-mahal-travel-tours.com/wonders-of-india/konark-sun-temple.html.

"Konark Sun Temple." Available online at http://templenet.com/Orissa/konark.html.

Library of Ancient Hindu History. Available online at http://www.hindunet.org/hindu_history/ancient_history.html.

Ludwig, Theodore. *The Sacred Paths.* Upper Saddle River, N.J.: Prentice Hall, 1996.

"Manipuri." Available online at *www.indiansaga.info/art/manipuri_dance.html.*

"Narada." Available online at *www.freeindia.org/biographies/sages/narada/* and *www.freeindia.org/biographies/sages/narada/page1.htm.*

Noss, David S. *A History of the World's Religions,* 11th ed. Upper Saddle River, N.J.: Prentice Hall, 2003.

"Nritya-Indian Classical Dance." Available online at *www.chandrakantha.com/articles/indian_music/* nritya.html

Oliver Craske/Genesis Publications. "Ravi Shankar." Available online at *www.eyeneer.com/Labels/Angel/* Ravi.html.

"Orissi." Available online at *www.indiansaga.info/art/orissi_dance.html.*

Smith, Huston. *The World's Religions: Our Great Wisdom Traditions.* San Francisco: Harper, 1991.

The Upanishads. Translated from the Sanskrit with an introduction by Juan Mascaro. London: Penguin Books Ltd., 1965.

FURTHER READING

PRIMARY SOURCES

Du Bary, William Theodore, et al. *Sources of the Indian Tradition.* New York: Columbia University Press, 1966.

Easwaran, Eknath, trans. *The Bhagavad Gita.* Tomales, Calif.: Nilgiri Press, 1985.

Fischer, Louis, ed. *The Essential Gandhi: An Anthology of His Writings on His Life, Work, and Ideas.* New York: Vintage Books, 2002.

Gandhi, Mohandas K. *The Bhagavad Gita According to Gandhi,* ed. John Strohmeier. Albany, Calif.: Berkeley Hills Books, 2000.

———. *Gandhi, An Autobiography: The Story of My Experiments with Truth.* Boston: Beacon Press, 1993.

Goodall, Dominic, ed. *Hindu Scriptures.* Berkeley, Calif.: University of California Press, 1996.

Harvey, Andrew, ed. *Teachings of the Hindu Mystics.* Boston: Shambhala, 2001.

Olivelle, Patrick, trans. *The Samnyasa Upanisads: Hindu Scriptures on Asceticism and Renunciation.* New York: Oxford University Press, 1992.

SECONDARY SOURCES

Breuilly, Elizabeth, Joanne O'Brien, and Martin Palmer. *Religions of the World.* Facts on File, Inc., 1997.

Dallapiccola, Anna. *Dictionary of Hindu Lore and Legend.* New York: Thames & Hudson, 2002.

Danielou, Alain. *The Myths and Gods of India: The Classic Work on Hindu Polytheism from the Princeton Bollingen Series.* Rochester, Vt.: Inner Traditions International Ltd., 1991.

Eck, Diana. *Darsan.* New York: Columbia University Press, 1998.

Frawley, David. *From the River of Heaven: Hindu and Vedic Knowledge for the Modern Age.* Twin Lakes, Wisc.: Lotus Press, 2000.

Herman, A.L. *A Brief Introduction to Hinduism: Religion, Philosophy, and Ways of Liberation.* Boulder, Colo.: Westview Press, 1991.

Hopkins, Thomas. *The Hindu Religion.* Belmont, Calif.: Dickenson Publishing Company, 1971.

Huyler, Steven P. *Meeting God: Elements of Hindu Devotion.* New Haven, Conn.: Yale University Press, 2002.

Knipe, David M. *Hinduism.* San Francisco: Harper, 1991.

Knott, Kim. *Hinduism: A Very Short Introduction.* New York: Oxford Press, 2000.

Lochtefeld, James G. *The Illustrated Encyclopedia of Hinduism.* New York: Rosen Publishing Group, 2002.

Michell, George. *The Hindu Temple: An Introduction to Its Meaning and Forms.* Chicago: University of Chicago Press, 1988.

Sharma, Arvind, ed. *Modern Hindu Thought: The Essential Texts.* New York: Oxford University Press, 2002.

Smith, David. *Hinduism and Modernity.* Malden, Mass.: Blackwell Publishers, 2003.

Sullivan, Bruce M. *A to Z of Hinduism.* Lanham, Md.: Scarecrow Press, 2001.

WEBSITES

BBC World Service Hinduism: An Introduction
http://www.bbc.co.uk/worldservice/people/features/world_religions/hinduism.shtml

Maintained by the British Broadcasting Corporation, this site provides an overview of Hindu beliefs and offers comparisons with other world religions.

FURTHER READING

Hinduism

http://www.religioustolerance.org/hinduism.htm

A site maintained by Religious Tolerance.org, it gives details about the history and beliefs of the world's third-largest religion.

Hindu Resources Online

http://www.hindu.org/

A site that aims to connect various Hindu organizations, leaders, and resources, informing the public about Hinduism-related news, events, and publications.

The Hindu Universe

http://www.hindunet.org/

Offers Hinduism-related information and links on everything from history and basic beliefs to astrology, current affairs, and social activities for Hindus.

Hindu Website

http://hinduwebsite.com/hinduindex.htm

Provides a broad overview of general Hindu history and beliefs and offers extensive links to further information about Hinduism available on the Internet.

John Howley and Spiritual Guides. "Hinduism." Available online at *www.vegetarian-restaurants.net/OtherInfo/Hindu.htm.*

Kamat, K.L. "Timeless Theater Art Archives." Available online at *www.kamat.com/kalranga/art/.*

Sacred-Texts: Hinduism

http://www.sacred-texts.com/hin/

Provides links to the full texts of a wide assortment of Hindu scriptures and literature.

Shankar, Ravi. "On Appreciation of Indian Classical Music." Available online at *www.ravishankar.org/indian_music_frame.html.*

INDEX

INDEX

INDEX

Page:

10: Chart adapted by the International Bulletin of Missionary Research, January 2003

B: © Victoria & Albert Museum, London/Art Resource, NY

B: © Giraudon/Art Resource, NY

C: © Charles & Josette Lenars/ CORBIS

C: © Paul Seheult; Eye Ubiquitous/ CORBIS

D: © Scala/Art Resource, NY

E: © Scala/Art Resource, NY

F: © Scala/Art Resource, NY

G: © Art Resource, NY

H: © Art Resource, NY

Cover: © Royalty-Free/CORBIS

CONTRIBUTORS

JAMES B. ROBINSON is a professor of religion at the University of Northern Iowa, where he has taught for thirty years. Born in Indianapolis, Indiana, he earned his undergraduate degree in philosophy and religion at Wabash College and attended graduate school at the University of Wisconsin-Madison. Dr. Robinson translated a series of stories about Buddhist magician saints, which was published as a book called *Buddha's Lions* by Dharma Publishing House in Berkeley, California.

ANN MARIE B. BAHR is professor of religious studies at South Dakota State University. Her areas of teaching, research, and writing include World Religions, New Testament, Religion in American Culture, and the Middle East. Her articles have appeared in *Annual Editions: World Religions 03/04* (Guilford, CT: McGraw-Hill, 2003), *The Journal of Ecumenical Studies*, and *Covenant for a New Creation: Ethics, Religion and Public Policy* (Maryknoll, NY: Orbis, 1991). Since 1999, she has authored a weekly newspaper column that analyzes the cultural significance of religious holidays. She has served as president of the Upper Midwest Region of the American Academy of Religion.

MARTIN E. MARTY, an ordained minister in the Evangelical Lutheran Church in America, is the Fairfax M. Cone Distinguished Service Professor Emeritus at the University of Chicago Divinity School, where he taught for thirty-five years. Marty has served as president of the American Academy of Religion, the American Society of Church History, and the American Catholic Historical Association, and was also a member of two U.S. presidential commissions. He is currently Senior Regent at St. Olaf College in Northfield, Minnesota. Marty has written more than fifty books, including the three-volume *Modern American Religion* (University of Chicago Press). His book *Righteous Empire* was a recipient of the National Book Award.